At the Firefly Gate

LINDA NEWBERY

Dolphin Paperbacks

First published in Great Britain in 2004
by Orion Children's Books
· This edition published 2005
by Dolphin paperbacks
a division of the Orion Publishing Group Ltd
Orion House
5 Upper St Martin's Lane
London WC2H 9EA

3 5 7 9 10 8 6 4 2

A catalogue record for this book is
available from the British Library.

Typeset at The Spartan Press Ltd,
Lymington, Hants

Printed in Great Britain by
Clays Ltd, St Ives plc

ISBN-10 1 84255 143 4
ISBN-13 978 1 84255 143 1

www.orionbooks.co.uk

To the children of St Mary's Primary School, Selly Oak

Contents

18th July 1943

*All day, he'd been unable to shake off a bad feeling
about tonight. It wasn't that he was superstitious – but
this was the thirteenth time, the thirteenth mission. He
wasn't superstitious, but he touched the wooden table
as he collected his parachute. He wasn't superstitious,
but he crossed the fingers of both hands as he walked
out to the airfield. If a black cat had walked across the
runway, that would have been even better. Not that
he was superstitious – of course not! But he would feel a
lot better when Number Thirteen was safely behind
him . . .*

ONE

Fireflies

It was the first night away from home. *This* was supposed to be home now, but it didn't feel like it. Henry stood looking out of his bedroom window into the dusk, at the fields, hedges and trees behind the cottage. In London there had always been traffic noise outside; here, he could almost feel the trees breathing. It was just past midsummer, and the sort of night that hardly got dark before the next early dawn.

As his eyes adjusted, Henry saw – with a thump of surprise – that someone was out there. A man, standing at the orchard gate.

The orchard was a narrow strip of grass and trees that ran behind the cottages, with a big field beyond. Each garden had a wooden gate at the end, so that you could walk straight out into the orchard. Henry's new garden was tangled and overgrown and by the end gate the strange man stood waiting – a young man, he looked, with a jacket slung over one shoulder. Henry saw points of light dancing around his head and shoulders.

They must be fireflies, he thought, straining his eyes: he'd heard of fireflies, but didn't know there really were such things. Among the dancing points of light, there was one small glow attached to the young man's hand: the tip of a lit cigarette. He was smoking, waiting.

What, or who, was he waiting for?

Watching him, Henry had the oddest sense of being both down there and up here. He could feel the floorboards under his bare feet and smell the dusty warmth of the bedroom, unused for so long. At the same time he smelled the coolness of grass and leaves, and felt the weight of the jacket on one shoulder and the wing-brush of insects against his face, and tasted the hot rush of smoke into his lungs. He saw the fireflies dance and flicker among the leaves of the apple trees, like tiny flames drawn by the glow of the cigarette.

And he knew that if he turned his head and looked up, he would see himself, a boy in blue pyjamas framed in the window, the light of the upstairs landing behind him.

4

He shook his head and the peculiar feeling vanished: he must have imagined it. But the young man hadn't vanished. He lifted his cigarette to his mouth, turned and looked straight at Henry.

He knows I'm here, Henry thought. *That's why he's standing there. Waiting.*

Quickly he ducked out of sight behind two packing-cases, even though he knew it was too late. Just for that second, the man had looked straight at him, without any sense of surprise, as if he'd expected to see a boy standing at the window. No, more than that: as if Henry were exactly the person he expected to see there.

Take deep breaths – in, out. Try to feel confident, then you'll be confident. That was what Dad said to do, when Henry got into a panic. But those panicky times were exactly when it was most impossible to breathe normally.

Henry turned and ran noisily downstairs, as if the thump of his feet would drive the stranger away. Mum was unpacking books while Dad made coffee in the small kitchen, the only room in any kind of order.

'There's a man outside!' Henry blurted. 'In the orchard, looking in.'

'At the end of our garden? It's OK, there's a public footpath runs along there,' Dad said. He opened the back door to look out. 'No. Can't see anyone.'

'He was by the gate, smoking.' Henry stepped out to the flagged path, which disappeared beneath a sprawl of nettles and thistles a few feet from the door. 'And there are *fireflies*.' He peered along the length of the garden. There was no young man, no fireflies, no cigarette-tip glowing in the dark – only the warm air and the breath of the trees.

'Just someone walking through,' Dad said, shepherding Henry back indoors. 'That footpath goes right along the orchard, then into the big field behind.'

He made it sound so ordinary. Less certain now of what he had seen, Henry couldn't explain the strangeness of it.

'Anyway,' Dad added, going back to the steaming kettle, 'you don't get fireflies, not in this country.'

'But I *saw* them!'

'Funny time to be out walking.' Mum was reaching deep into a crate, head down, bottom up. 'Hen, it's time for bed. You've had a long day.'

'Mu-um! Don't call me Hen!'

'Sorry,' Mum said, from inside the box. 'I'll come up in a minute to see you've got everything you need.'

'Curtains,' Henry said. 'I haven't got curtains.'

6

'I know.' Mum straightened up. 'We'll find them tomorrow. Won't matter, will it, not for one night? This time of year it's only dark for a few hours and you're at the back of the house. It's not as if anyone can see in.'

But the man outside!

'Night, Henry. Sleep tight,' Dad said, as he always did.

Henry went upstairs and crept to the window to check again, but saw only the twisted trunks of the apple trees and their shadowy leaves in the dusk. The man *wasn't* walking, he thought; he was waiting for something. Or for someone. He was waiting for *me*.

And, in the room that held all the day's warmth, he felt a cold shiver between his shoulder-blades, like iced water trickling.

TWO

Hen

3, Church Cottages, Crickford St. Thomas, Suffolk, was the sort of address Henry's mum had always wanted. Henry knew she had dreamed of moving to a village like this.

Their cottage, one of four in a row near the church, had stood empty for nearly a year. Going in was like opening up those boxes that fit one inside the other. From the front it looked tiny and narrow, with a door so low that Dad had to duck his head to get through. Inside, there was a series of rooms like a tunnel, finally reaching the kitchen and back door, which led to a long thin garden.

'Right,' said Dad on the second day, rubbing his hands. 'That's the moving over and done with. Now we start living here.'

'Over and done with?' Mum turned slowly one

way and then the other, surveying the muddle and the boxes still waiting to be unpacked. 'I don't think so!'

It was another day of sorting, of wondering where things were, of trying to find places for everything. 'Soon be back to normal,' Dad kept saying, clambering over rolled-up carpet, or un-ravelling a tangle of wire flex, or trying to find a handful of screws that matched. He'd had to drive ten miles to the nearest DIY shop for curtain hooks, two tins of paint and an extension lead.

Normal! He must be joking, Henry thought. As far as he could see, nothing would ever be normal again. *Normal* was their old flat. *Normal* was run-ning downstairs to Nabil's, playing football in the park or going to the newsagent's for crisps or cho-colate. *Normal* was school – Strawberry Hill Primary and Mr Greenstreet, who taught class 6G and or-ganised the football teams. Henry was missing the last week-and-a-bit of Year Six, the days full of fun things and a party before leaving primary school for ever and moving up to Fuller's Wood, the com-prehensive. Now, instead of going there with Nabil and his other friends, he'd have to start at an unknown school, Hartsfield High, without a single friend. It was weeks away, but still he had a sick, blurry feeling every time he thought about it.

Mum and Dad thought it was great, moving. But Henry couldn't see much point in Mum moving miles away from London only to travel back there every day to work. Even Dad's new job in Ipswich was half-an-hour's drive away. Grown-ups were always going on about common-sense, without noticing how short of it they were themselves. And Henry *liked* London; it was what he was used to. He liked the mazy streets and the Underground and the red buses. He liked the parks and the pavement art and the pigeons. He liked the Planetarium and the London Eye and the Science Museum. Nabil's mum and dad were museum fanatics, and were working their way round all of them with the two boys.

Henry thought of exploring, running out across the fields and finding a stream, a wood, trees to climb. But there was one important thing missing: a friend. It wouldn't be much fun doing that sort of thing on his own. He wanted Nabil to live here too.

'You can have Nabil to stay in the holidays,' Mum told him. It was weird how she sometimes did that – picked up what he was thinking, as if he'd spoken aloud. 'Moving away doesn't mean you can't still be friends.'

'But it won't be the *same*,' Henry complained.

'Things don't stay the same for ever,' Mum said. 'They change, they move on. There's email, there are phones, you could even write Nabil a *letter*. Come on, I've found your curtains at last. Let's get them hung.'

Henry hadn't slept well last night with the black blank of the window and the thought of the strange man outside. It all seemed so different in daylight that by now he wasn't sure why it had bothered him – someone on the footpath, stopping for a rest and a smoke, that was all. He liked his new room: the way it jutted out at the back of the house and its three steps up from the landing, which seemed to set it apart from the rest. The floor was uneven and creaked when he walked on it, so that crossing from door to window felt like being in a boat. When Mum had finished in here, he was going to put up his Chelsea posters and drape his scarf along the curtain rail. Then the room would seem more like his.

He leaned on the window-sill and saw Dad outside with a sickle, hacking a path from door to back gate. The garden must have been left to grow wild for years. According to Dad, it was unexplored jungle and might harbour creatures like pythons, orang-utans and two-toed sloths. He saw Henry watching and called up: 'Send a search-party if I don't come back for lunch. Tell them to bring survival rations and snake-bite serum!'

'It'll be more like your old room, with these up.'
Mum was standing on a chair, mumbling through
the curtain-hook she held between her lips. 'And
you won't have to imagine there's someone out
there.'

'I *didn't* imagine!' Henry retorted; but the memory of the waiting man had faded so shadowily that
he couldn't be sure.

'Count me out another five hooks, can you, Hen?
See that box there? I need this sort, not the comma-
shaped ones.' Mum held one out to show him.

'Mum, don't call me Hen!'

'Sorry, I keep forgetting.'

'Well, *don't* forget!'

He hated being called Hen. It wasn't so bad at
home, but suppose she said it when someone was
listening – someone from his new school? He'd be
called Hen for ever. It made him feel like a little
clucking chicken.

'Soon as you go to school next week,' Mum said,
'you'll make friends, and then you won't feel so
strange.'

She'd done it again! Picked up his thought. Not
that there was any chance of her forgetting. It was
all arranged – he was joining Year Six at the village
school just for two days, to visit Hartsfield High
with them, the comprehensive.

12

'What's the point?' he asked, knowing it was useless. 'Why don't I wait till September?'

'Why does it feel like we've had this conversation before?' Mum said, draping the curtain over her arm. 'Could it be that we *have,* five times at least? You wouldn't want to miss going to Hartsfield with the others—'

Yes, I would, Henry thought.

'—it'll help you feel much less new when you start there in September – and you can start making friends in the village. You will, Henry!'

Henry shook his head obstinately. 'What was the problem with staying on at home till school breaks up? I could have stayed at Nabil's.'

'*This* is home now,' said Mum. 'You'll see Nabil in the holidays, and by then you'll be feeling a lot happier. I promise.'

Henry chased a spider through the open window and watched it lower itself down the outside wall by a thread.

'Pat's daughter's about your age. Oh, that reminds me,' Mum said, looking at her watch. 'I said we'd all call round later, just to say hello. Pat's going to keep an eye on you, when I'm at work next week.'

'Why does she need to?' Henry asked, though they'd had this conversation before, too. He'd been embarrassed to hear Mum discussing *child-care arrangements,* as she called them, with Pat, their new neighbour; it made him sound like a two-year-old in a pushchair. 'Can't you just give me a door key?'

'You'll have a door key, but you'll be spending some time at Pat's. I expect you and Grace'll soon be friends.'

'Amazing Grace?' Henry said, thinking of the song they sang in assembly sometimes, back at Strawberry Hill.

'We'll find out.'

Later, on the doorstep of Number One, Mum squeezed his arm. 'It's OK, we won't embarrass you. Henry, not Hen! Not a single Hen will pass our lips. Remember!' she added sternly to Dad, although *she* was the one most likely to forget.

The front door opened. And within five minutes of meeting Grace, Henry knew they would never be friends. Not if she had her way. Not if he had his way, either.

THREE

Grace

Inside Number One, the rooms were arranged exactly as in Henry's house, with the front door opening straight into the main room and the stairs coming down in the middle. Pat seemed nice – a bit older than Mum, and shorter and plumper. Her husband, John, was so big that he and Dad between them seemed to fill the whole space with their tallness. Henry felt even smaller than usual.

'Grace! Come down and say hello!' Pat had to yell upstairs three times before Grace stomped down. She was a long stretch taller than Henry, skinny, with tanned legs in cycle shorts. She had fair hair that flopped into her eyes; pushing it back, she looked at Henry as if it hadn't been worth the effort of coming all the way downstairs for someone so uninteresting.

'Grace is at Hartsfield too,' Pat said. 'So from September you can get the bus together and Grace can help you settle in and make friends. It's a lovely school, isn't it, Gracie? We're very happy with it.'

She smiled at everyone; Grace kicked at the skirting board. The way Pat spoke, Henry thought, was as if Grace had been all sunny and smiling.

'I'll be in Year Eight,' Grace said sulkily to the stair carpet. She stood with one foot still on the second step, as if she couldn't wait to bolt back upstairs. 'I won't have much to do with Year Sevens.'

'Bit of a change, isn't it?' Pat said to Henry. 'Don't worry – you'll be fine. You'll soon make friends here. Grace can help you find your way around. Can't you, Gracie?' she added, in a tougher voice than before, so that it sounded like a warning.

Grace made a grunting noise, gave up trying to escape upstairs and plugged herself into a Walkman, slumping into a chair with her long legs dangling over one of its arms.

'It'll be nice for Henry to have a friend,' said Mum, who also seemed oblivious of Grace's fierce scowl. 'To know someone already.'

Huh! Henry thought. He wasn't going to hang around with a sulky girl who obviously wanted

16

nothing to do with him. They must think him so amazingly dim that he'd wander off and get lost without Grace to show him where to go.

'Let's go outside. It's so nice and sunny.' Pat led the way through the kitchen. 'We've got my aunt staying with us for a bit. Dottie.'

Following, Henry thought for a moment that she meant the aunt *was* dotty, but then Pat called out, 'Dottie! Our new neighbours are here,' and he realised that it was her name. He glanced back to see if Grace was coming out too, but she stayed in her chair, not even looking up.

Outside, the sunlight was so bright that it made him squint. A trowel and a plastic tray of pansies lay on the grass; someone had dug over a patch of earth ready to plant them. In the shade of the fence, in a garden chair, sat a very old lady. She was small and frail and so thin that her weight in the fabric seat seemed no more than a moth's.

Pat introduced Mum and Dad. The lady shook hands with them and said, 'Pleased to meet you,' in an old, cracked voice.

'And this is Henry,' Pat said, giving him a gentle push.

The old lady seemed surprised by the name. She stared at him hard, as if she wanted to make quite sure who he was. Then she smiled and said, 'Henry.'

17

Just that. The way she smiled made him think she knew him already. Her eyes, in a brown, lined face, were amazingly blue and clear, as if a much younger, stronger person were looking out of the frail body.

'She's been ill,' Henry heard Pat explaining to Mum and Dad in a low voice as they moved to the end of the garden. 'She's got a flat in Ipswich, but she can't manage on her own any more.'

Mum made a sympathetic noise, then said, 'What a gorgeous garden! It'll take a lot of work to get ours anything like this.'

There were roses and flowers, not a weed or a thistle in sight, and the lawn was smooth and green. Henry thought of their own jungle-slice. The only similarity was that both gardens had a wooden gate leading out to the orchard behind. While the others talked, he stood at the gate looking out at the trees and wondering how long it would be before they grew apples. One or two of them would be good to climb, he decided. He didn't know who the orchard belonged to, but Dad had said there was a public footpath, so there was nothing to stop him going in. Again he thought of the man who'd stood there last night, with the dancing fireflies. It hadn't been John; the smoking man had been slimmer and younger, as well as

18

nowhere near as tall. Anyway, why would John stand *there*, by someone else's back gate? Whatever the grown-ups said about footpaths, it was suspicious. If he saw that man again he was going to sneak up on him – which would be much easier now that Dad had slashed a path down the garden – and find out exactly what he was up to.

'Well, it's time we went back and did something about lunch,' Mum was saying, and Dad added, 'We're still a bit chaotic, indoors. It'll be a relief to go back to work tomorrow, I can tell you.'

'Bye then, Henry,' Dottie called from her chair. 'See you tomorrow!' Again that look – as if she'd known him for ages, as if they were great friends and could have had a good old natter if there'd been more time. Just for a second, as he smiled back, he felt like that, too.

They went through the house to the front door. Grace was nowhere to be seen. Mum and Dad must have noticed how rude she was. She could hardly have made it more obvious that she wanted nothing to do with him.

But all Dad said, opening their own front door, was, 'Nice family, aren't they? Did I get round to putting any beer in the fridge?'

FOUR

Left Out

Henry knew, with a part of his mind, that he was in bed and dreaming. But the dream was so real that he could smell the crushed grass and the doughnuts and feel the sun hot on his face.

He was in a line of people – all young men his own age – waiting at the serving hatch of a mobile café. Standing in line, he felt in his pocket for change.

Rusty nudged him. 'Hey up! She's a nice change from old Mike, I'll say that for her.'

Henry looked, and saw a girl at the counter, beside Mike who was always there. She had wavy brown hair clipped back from her face; she wasn't especially pretty, but had amazingly blue, blue eyes that seemed to take in everything. She wore a yellow blouse and, over it, a clean white apron.

When she crossed to the urn to top up a teapot with boiling water, her movements were full of energy. She turned back and just for a second looked straight at Henry, giving him a quick, shy smile. He was too slow to smile back. He felt himself going scarlet.

The lad at the front of the queue must have made a joke; she burst out laughing. She had the most wonderful laugh Henry had ever heard. It rippled up from inside her and made him want to join in, even though he hadn't heard what the boy said.

'She'll cheer up our tea-breaks, eh?' Rusty said in his ear.

'What you got for us today then, love?' the next person asked.

'Rock cakes, doughnuts, currant buns, fresh from the oven,' the girl recited, in a Cockney accent. 'And Mike's special doorstop cheese sandwiches.'

Henry couldn't take his eyes off her.

'Tea and a doughstop – I mean, tea and a doughnut, please,' he asked shyly, when it was his turn. He knew he was still blushing.

'That'll be tuppence,' the girl said. Henry handed over his shilling and she counted out his change – a sixpence, two pennies and four ha'pennies. As he

21

took the coins from her he managed to drop them, scattering them on the grass.

'Sorry,' he and the girl said, both at once.

He bent to pick them up, conscious of how daft he must look, bum in the air, scrabbling around after the glint of silver and copper in the grass. When all the coins were safely in his hand he straightened and smiled, and the girl looked relieved. 'I'm such a clumsy ha'porth!' she said. 'It's my first day, see – all fingers and thumbs, I am! See you tomorrow, then!' And she smiled directly at him before whisking round to the caddy to spoon fresh tea-leaves into the pot.

The doughnut was large and sticky and the tea was strong, in a chipped enamel mug. Carrying them, Henry walked slowly away, turning to look back at the girl as he waited for Rusty. Rusty said something to her and she smiled politely, but it wasn't the special smile she'd given Henry.

'Hey up, Hen!' Rusty said, catching up. He nudged Henry with his elbow, as his hands were taken up with a tea-mug and two doughnuts. 'She's taken a bit of a shine to you, if you ask me! *See you tomorrow*! It's practically a date!'

'Don't be daft,' Henry said. 'And leave off calling me Hen, will you!'

They sat down on the grass. Henry's change was

still in his hand; about to put it in his trouser pocket, he glanced down and saw that the sixpenny-bit was a shiny new one. He liked those – they were meant to be lucky if you got one in your portion of Christmas pudding. 'Here,' he said on an impulse, handing it to Rusty. 'This is for you. For luck.'

'What, really?' said Rusty. 'Tea and a doughnut on me this afternoon, then.'

'No. Don't spend it,' Henry said. 'Keep it. Keep it safe.'

It seemed important; he didn't know why. But the dream was fading, the voices far away, and he was looking at bright daylight filtered through his bedroom curtains. He'd been about to bite into that doughnut and his throat was dry, thirsting for the tea.

Sometimes Henry had a dream so vivid that he didn't want to leave it, and this was one. He lay there thinking about it. Rusty? He'd never heard the name before, but could still see the freckled face and the thatch of ginger hair. He didn't know why, but that grinning face seemed as familiar as Nabil's, as if Rusty were his best friend. And he knew that Rusty's name was Rusty Dobbs and that he came from Lowestoft and had a younger brother who walked with a limp because he'd had polio. All that must have been in the dream, though Henry couldn't remember dreaming it. And it was weird about the girl, because Henry didn't much like girls, but he liked the one at the canteen – her smile and her friendliness – and felt sorry that she was only in a dream.

Funny, too – in the dream he had seemed to be older, though he felt just the same inside . . . but the memory was dissolving before he could clutch at any more detail, and the reality of Today was taking over. Stacked in the corner facing him were the boxes he'd got to unpack today. There was a crack in the plaster that snaked down from the ceiling. Dad, suddenly a DIY enthusiast, had said he'd soon repair it, and that Henry could choose any colour he liked for the walls. Chelsea blue was what Henry had in mind.

All the days had got a bit jumbled, and Henry had to cast about in his mind before remembering that it was Monday. No school, because he wouldn't be going in until tomorrow, for the first of the introductory days at Hartsfield High. It felt like a big weight in his chest, the thought of facing a class full of people he didn't know, and everyone staring. He'd get a whole new lot of teasing, he knew he would, about his smallness. But he needn't let that spoil today. He had a day's free holiday, and the sun was already shining with such confidence that it seemed no rain cloud would dare get in its way for weeks to come.

It was so quiet here. At home in London he had woken to the rumble of traffic on the road outside. Here, he heard one solitary car in the village street and birds singing, and – yes! A cuckoo! The first he'd ever heard, but unmistakable. He went to the window and looked out at the garden, the orchard trees, the field beyond, all hazy and soft in the early light. Cuck-oo! There it was again, a long way off – from the wood on the other side of the wheatfield.

'Cuck-oo!' he called back at it, waited and heard the answer float across the field a few moments later.

He splashed some water over his face, brushed his teeth and put on his jeans and a T-shirt. Dad had gone off to Ipswich, early, to start his new job, and Mum would be back at work tomorrow. Henry had often wondered how his parents could be so different when it came to tidiness and order: Dad, like Henry, was the sort of person who scattered belongings around the house – a book here, a sweater there – and was forever looking for things he'd misplaced. Mum, on the other hand, was meticulous about tidiness. *A place for everything and everything in its place* was her motto and her mission in the new house was to decide just where those places ought to be. While Henry ate his Shreddies, she finished arranging the herbs and spices in alphabetical order, then began ironing next day's clothes. While Henry put an extra slice of bread in the toaster, she began next day's ironing. She made short work of a crisp white shirt for Dad and a lilac one for herself; then, Henry saw with foreboding, his own, bright-red Strawberry Hill sweatshirt, with its printed strawberry design.

'You can wear this tomorrow,' she explained. 'The letter said you should wear uniform.'

'It didn't mean Strawberry Hill uniform! I'll be the only one!'

'Well, we'll see,' Mum conceded. 'It might be too hot for a sweatshirt. But I've washed and ironed it just in case. Now, are you going to start on those boxes?'

It was odd, but having a day off school wasn't as much fun as he'd expected. He sorted out his room - his books, models, CDs and some games he was really too old for, which he shoved out of the way in the bottom of his wardrobe – and it was still only halfway through the morning. He wandered

26

downstairs. Mum had finished ironing and was now marshalling pots of jam, marmalade, mustard and pickle into one of the top cupboards. The back door was open, and on the mat, watching her with an expression of great seriousness, was a black-and-white cat with long white whiskers. It gave Henry a haughty look, then – obviously not much impressed – began licking one of its front paws, curving its wrist delicately.

'Whose is that?'

'The cat?' Mum turned to check. 'No idea. Pat's, maybe? It just strolled in as if it belongs here.'

Henry liked cats. 'Shall we give it some milk?'

'Yes. I mean no, we're nearly out. You could go and buy some from the village shop, if they've got it? And a loaf of bread.'

She gave Henry a two-pound coin. Outside, he broke into a run, past the row of cottages to the village green. The primary school was on the nearest side, the Post Office shop on the farther. It was playtime; everyone was out in the railed playground at the front. A football slammed against the wall and a boy ran over for it, grinning, while others called for attention; a girl yelled to another girl; smaller children crouched over games at ground level. The boy controlled the ball and looked around, deciding who to kick it to, then passed to a ginger-headed boy who dribbled neatly past two others before booting it between rucksack-goalposts by the far wall.

'Yes! Yes!' he crowed, arms held high, while one of the others protested, 'That was off-side, just now!'

None of them noticed Henry as he slowed to watch. A teacher came out of the main door with a bell – an old-fashioned hand-bell – which she clanged loudly. Still arguing about the off-side rule, the boys drifted inside, following the smaller children. The school was tiny: a stone building with its own clock-tower, high windows each side of the main door and two mobile classrooms at the edge of the playground. It looked friendly. But Henry had finished with primary school now; he'd already left it behind. At the moment, he belonged nowhere.

Feeling lonely and left out, he crossed the grass towards the shop. At Strawberry Hill, the seat next to Nabil's would be empty. What would they be doing now, in class 6G? He felt a pang of home-sickness that was like tummy-ache.

For the rest of the day he helped Mum to empty and flatten the remaining boxes and to put every-thing in cupboards and drawers. The cat lapped its milk, then curled up on the sofa. 'It'll leave hairs,'

Mum said, not used to animals in the house, but Henry pleaded for the cat to be allowed to stay. Later, he found it settled comfortably on his bed. It seemed to have moved in. It was a smart-looking cat, glossy black, with a white shirt-front, bristly white whiskers and white forepaws that looked dipped in milk. Its green eyes watched Henry lazily.

'Can we keep it?' he asked Mum when he next went downstairs.

'Of course not! It must belong to someone, a well-fed cat like that. Doesn't look like a stray, to me. I'll ask Pat.'

At that moment there was a knock on the front door. Henry went to answer and found Grace, leaning against the wall of the porch. She was in school uniform: short grey skirt, untucked white shirt and clumpy black shoes.

'Mum says d'you want to come round,' she said, without looking at him.

Henry opened his mouth to say no thanks, but Mum was there first. 'That's kind of you!' she exclaimed, as if the idea had been Grace's own. 'Do you mean just Henry, or both of us?'

Grace examined her fingernails. 'Whatever.'

'Actually I really ought to stay and finish this. Can you explain to your mum? But Henry can come. It's been a bit dull for him, all day sorting

29

stuff out. And', Mum added, ushering him out of the door, 'you can ask about the cat. Go on, Henry.' At least she didn't call him Hen.

Grace turned away with a *suit yourself* shrug. Reluctantly, Henry followed.

FIVE

Pudding

Henry wouldn't have admitted it to anyone, not even to Nabil, but he was scared of girls.

Not *all* girls. Some – like Zubaida and Winifred and Antonina, in his class at Strawberry Hill – were OK. But there was a particular kind of girl he had learned to fear. Older girls. Loud girls. Girls who huddled together in scornful, cackling groups. Girls like Grace. Not that he'd actually seen Grace doing any of that, not yet, but her sulky voice and snooty expression warned him that she could huddle and cackle with the worst of them.

Back in London there had been four Year Eight girls who always stood in the door of the video shop when he was on his way home from school. It was bad enough when he was with Nabil; worse every Wednesday, when Nabil went to his auntie's and Henry had to go home on his own.

'Oh, isn't he *cute*!' they'd call out, loudly enough for everyone in the street to hear.

'Look at his sweet little face! Ickle Henrykins!'

'Are you a trial size? A free sample?'

'Watch out, Henrykins. Leanne gobbles up little boys for breakfast.'

'Yeah, and big boys for dinner!' Titter, giggle, shove.

'Hey, I bet—' And they would go into one of their whispering huddles, emerging from it with whoops and cackles that made Henry go scarlet as he scuttled past. That only provoked more taunts.

'Ah, look, we've embarrassed him!'

'Look at his little face! Matches his sweatshirt!'

'*Sssssss!*'

'Hurry home to Mummy – infants like you shouldn't be out on your own!'

When Henry had tried to tell Dad about it, he couldn't make it sound nearly as bad as it felt. 'Answer them back!' Dad advised. 'Don't let them get to you. Anyway, you won't always be small. When I was a year or two older than you, I suddenly shot up about a foot, in a matter of weeks. They'll soon drop it and start on someone else.'

'Good things come in small packages,' Mum would say, ruffling his hair.

Back in their London flat, there were pencil-marks on his bedroom wall to show his height, each line with a date written neatly beside. Although the marks were creeping up the wall, it wasn't nearly fast enough to keep up with the rest of Year Six. Nabil, for instance, seemed to grow two or three centimetres for every one of Henry's. Mum and Dad were always assuring him that he'd catch up eventually, but *eventually* seemed to be a long time coming.

Now, unwillingly, Henry trudged behind Grace to Number One. At the front gate she paused, and told him, in her throwaway manner, 'You can talk to dotty Aunt Dottie in the garden, Midget. I've got things to do.'

'She didn't seem dotty.' Henry thought of the old lady's bright eyes and her friendliness. 'Not to me.'

Grace shrugged. 'Well, ill then. I mean, *really* ill. That's why she looks so incredibly old. I bet you thought she was a hundred, didn't you? Well, she's not.'

She pushed open the front gate. Pat was there at the door, smiling and cheerful in a bright yellow T-shirt with a blue whale on the front. 'Come on through. We're just having some tea.'

They went through the kitchen to the garden. A table and chairs were set out there, and washing on a spinner. The old lady was sitting in her padded chair, just like yesterday, having a cup of tea and a game of Scrabble with Pat. She smiled at Henry and said, 'Henry. It's Henry,' as if she liked saying his name; as if he were the person she had most been hoping to see. Henry looked at her, thinking of what Grace had just said. Dottie couldn't be *that* ill, could she? Or she'd be indoors, in bed.

Pat brought Coke and cake for Henry and refilled Dottie's tea-cup. Dottie took a piece of cake too – a big piece – and said to Henry, 'How's things? Getting yourselves straight along there?'

Wondering how long he ought to stay, he took a gulp of Coke, too quickly; the bubbles fizzed up his nose, making him sneeze.

'Bless you!' said Dottie, and laughed. Henry's wariness vanished as he looked at her, before another sneeze exploded out of him. She had an amazing laugh, rippling up from somewhere deep inside her, and she grinned at him as if she knew exactly what it was like to have Coke bubbles up her nose.

'You going to play on the computer?' Pat said to Grace. 'Henry might like to join you.'

34

Grace shook her head. She stuffed cake into her mouth until her cheeks bulged like a hamster's, then sprawled on the grass, facing away from everyone, to read a magazine.

Remembering the cat, Henry told Pat and Dottie about it. 'It's not yours, is it?'

Pat shook her head. 'No, we haven't got a cat – John's allergic to their fur. But from what you say, it sounds like Pudding, though it's hard to believe after so long.'

'Pudding?' Henry echoed. The cat at home seemed far too dignified to be called Pudding.

'Pudding belonged to the old man who lived in your house – Mr Jessop,' Pat said. 'Over a year ago he moved out, to a nursing home, and the house was empty from then till it was put up for sale and your Mum and Dad bought it. His son and daughter-in-law were going to take the cat because the nursing home had a No Pets rule. But he was nowhere to be found. They searched and searched, put notices up in the shop and on lamp-posts, but not a sign of Pudding. Seemed he'd wandered off.'

'Cats sense things,' said Dottie. 'Sounds like he knew things was about to change, so he made his own arrangements. That's cats for you. Independent.'

Pat nodded. 'I've got Jim Jessop's phone number

indoors somewhere - that's Mr Jessop's son. He'll be pleased to know Pudding's turned up, if it *is* Pudding. White whiskers, you said? Two white paws? Must be. After all this time – well, I never!'

Henry was disappointed, thinking of the cat sitting smugly on his bed, as if they'd come to an agreement to share the room. He didn't want Jim Jessop to come and take the cat away. He wanted it for his own.

Dottie looked at him. 'Sounds like Pudding wants to move in with you!'

'I remember hearing old Mr Jessop calling him in, last thing at night,' Pat said. ' "*Puss – Puss – Pudding*!" he'd call, like that. Nine o'clock on the dot, he'd open the back door – you could set your watch by him. Nine o'clock, on the dot, "*Puss – Puss – Pudding*!" '

Grace made a *phuh* sound – somewhere between a scornful laugh and a snort of disgust – and got abruptly to her feet. She went indoors, leaving her magazine on the grass.

'You can go in too if you like,' Pat told Henry. 'I knew it wouldn't be long before she was on the Internet. It's John's computer really, but we've had to put it in Grace's room, up in the attic – there's no space for it otherwise. She spends more time on it than he does. Go on up. She won't mind.'

Henry shook his head. Grace *would* mind; it was obvious. If she'd been nicer, he might have asked if he could email Nabil; the computer at home wouldn't be connected to the Internet till a phone engineer came to put in a new socket. But Grace could hardly have signalled more clearly that she didn't want to be bothered with him.

He felt awkward and in the way. Was it too soon to go home or would that look rude? But Grace was far ruder and no one seemed to notice. He glanced at the magazine she'd left on the grass, expecting something girly about clothes and pop groups and make-up. Instead, to his surprise, it was *Fighter Pilot*, with a picture of a Eurofighter on the front. He wouldn't have minded borrowing that himself.

'That's what Gracie wants to be when she grows up.' Dottie saw him looking at it.

'What?'

'A fighter pilot,' said Pat. 'Funny, she's had that idea in her head since she was about five. I wonder if she'll end up too tall, though, if she takes after her Dad.'

'But—'

'Girls can be fighter pilots, you know,' Dottie told him, with a touch of sternness. She seemed as good as Mum at guessing what he was thinking.

And what Henry was thinking now was that Grace was the oddest girl he'd ever met.

'In her dreams,' he felt like saying; but Dottie picked up that thought, too.

'We all have our dreams, don't we?' she said. 'Even at my age.' She laughed her infectious laugh that reminded Henry of someone else, and tapped the side of her head. 'You wouldn't believe what silly old nonsense goes on in here!'

SIX

Strawberry

To Henry's disappointment, Pudding – or the cat that resembled Pudding – was nowhere to be seen when he went back home, and did not return for the rest of the evening.

'Early to bed for you,' Mum told him, soon after the dishes had been cleared away from supper. Having spent all day shelving and sorting, she was now back into Work Routine, which meant that everything had to be organised and ready by bedtime: three packed lunches in Tupperware containers in the fridge, everyone's shoes shined, her briefcase by the front door, ironed shirts on hangers and Henry's rucksack packed with everything he might need during the day, from sharpened pencils to clean PE kit. No wonder Dad called her his Personal Organiser.

In the morning it had turned cool. Henry put on his Strawberry Hill sweatshirt over a plain white T-shirt, planning to take it off as soon as he could. Mum had to leave at 7:15 for her train and it was Dad who walked with Henry to the primary school. Henry felt himself shrinking beside Dad, growing even smaller as they approached the railings. They were so early that there was no one in the play-ground.

'You'll have a good day,' Dad told him. 'Don't worry – just be yourself! People are sure to like you.'

But why should they, Henry wondered? They'll all have their own friends already. They won't want to bother with me.

'Ah, yes. Henry Stirling? Miss Murphy's expecting you,' said a secretary in the tiny office inside. She checked his name against a list. 'She's in the classroom on the left.'

Miss Murphy was standing on a desk, pinning paintings to the wall. She was younger than Henry had expected, and wore smart black trousers, a striped T-shirt and trainers. Her auburn hair was cut very short; she had a small pointy face and an easy smile. Henry felt better as they all introduced themselves.

Dad stayed chatting for a few moments, while Henry looked around the room. The back wall was a mosaic of artwork – collages, prints, drawings and paintings. There was a coloured drawing of a frog that Henry thought particularly good; looking closely, he read the pencilled name *Simon Dobbs*.

People started to come into the room – excited, jostling, looking curiously at Dad and at Henry. They all wore dark-green sweatshirts with an oak leaf emblem. Among them Henry recognised the grinning boy and the ginger-headed one he'd seen playing football in the playground. Dad said his goodbyes and left. Before Henry had time to feel like an abandoned infant, Miss Murphy clapped her hands and told them it was time to go out to the coach.

'We'll be sitting in the front seats,' she told them, 'so don't go diving for the back. Henry's joining us today – he's just moved to the village and he'll be starting Year Seven at Hartsfield High just like the rest of you, so I hope you'll help him feel at home. Henry, you can sit next to Simon on the coach. Simon, come and say hello.'

'Hi, Henry.' Henry looked into the friendly, freckled face of the ginger-haired boy. How had he guessed that this must be Simon?

'The boy Simon usually sits with – Tim – will be going to Stowmarket next year, not Hartsfield,'

Miss Murphy explained, 'so Simon's without a partner.'

'Great frog,' Henry said, gesturing towards the wall. To his surprise, Simon's face went red, and he mumbled, 'Thanks. What team d'you support?'

'Chelsea,' Henry told him, adding, as Simon obviously wanted to be asked, 'You?'

'Norwich. The Canaries. Where d'you live, then?'

'Just off the green. Three, Church Cottages.'

Simon nodded. 'Near Grace.'

'Do you know her?'

'Everyone knows Grace,' Simon said, grinning.

As they followed Miss Murphy out into the playground and on to the street, Henry had the odd feeling that he'd talked to Simon before. Puzzling, he fell silent. Next moment he had a nasty surprise – there was Grace, waiting for the coach with a group of others in the grey uniform of Hartsfield High.

'Midget!' she called out. 'What's that you're wearing?' She nodded towards Henry's scarlet sweatshirt.

His cheeks burned; he'd forgotten to take it off. 'It's my uniform. From my old school.' Everyone had worn red sweatshirts at his old school, so no one thought there was anything hilariously funny about them. But he didn't want to stand out like an enormous over-ripe strawberry, not on his first day.

Grace giggled. 'OK if you don't mind looking like a great squidgy dollop of strawberry jam. Or a walking advert for Pick-Your-Own.'

'So what?' Simon said. 'Better than grungey grey, isn't it?'

Grace's chin jutted. 'Who asked you, Gingernut?'

'Who asked you, Stringbean?'

'Now, now,' said Miss Murphy. 'We'll have none of that on the bus, thank you very much.'

The coach pulled up and she made the older pupils stand back to let the Year Sixes on first. In London, coaches had only been for special outings; it would feel odd to travel to school in one every day. Seated next to Simon, Henry was about to pull his sweatshirt over his head, when he realised that Grace would know he'd minded what she said. He decided to keep it on.

Hartsfield High, twenty minutes away, looked enormous. With its drive, vast playing fields and a bewildering number of buildings, it looked to Henry like a small town. Here, the Year Sixes were told to stay in their seats while the older children got off the coach first; and as Grace passed Henry, she hissed *'Strawberry Pip!'* in his ear.

Fortunately, he didn't see her for the rest of the

43

day – apart from glimpsing her once across the big canteen at lunchtime. The group from Crickford St. Thomas were to be divided among six different form groups, joining children from various other primary schools, but Henry was relieved to find that he and Simon were together, in 7JM.

First, there was an assembly with the Head Teacher; next, a tour of the whole school and a sort of treasure hunt with clues to follow; then sessions with various subject teachers, finishing with a team construction game to see who could build the strongest bridge out of cardboard.

It felt like being in a small, vulnerable flock – shepherded from place to place, not allowed to stray, while older pupils looked at them with mild interest. What would it be like when they had to manage on their own? Some of the teenagers he saw around the place were huge – twice Henry's size at least. As for the sixth-formers: some of them were so grown-up, and some of the teachers so young, that it was hard to tell the difference, especially as the sixth form didn't wear uniform.

As they were led from the Main Hall to the Science Block, they passed a big gang of teenagers clustered around one of the mobile classrooms. 'Year Tens,' said Simon, who had an older cousin at the school. One of the girls went, 'Aaah – sweet little things!' to her friend, looking mainly at Henry, with a soppy smile on her face. It reminded him uncomfortably of Leanne and her group. He was doomed to be Cute Little Henrykins wherever he went! His only hope was to hide himself in a cluster of others - or to put on a growing spurt over the summer holidays.

The day seemed to go on for ever. On the coach home, everyone was talking at once about which form tutor they had and which sessions they'd enjoyed or found confusing. By now Henry knew quite a few names – there was Jonathan and Neil and Andrew and Elissa, whose hair was in a single plait right down to her bottom, and Jenny, who had a brace on her teeth. He'd taken off his Strawberry Hill sweater at morning break and stuffed it in his rucksack, so there were no more remarks about it from Grace, but she waited for him when everyone piled off the coach outside the village school.

'You're coming home with me,' she told him. 'Mum said.'

'Same time tomorrow, everyone!' Miss Murphy reminded Year Six. 'And remember you'll need PE kit.'

'See you tomorrow, Henry!' Simon called, and ran off towards a car waiting for him across the green – he lived in a different village.

Following Grace, Henry noticed the *Fighter Pilot* magazine poking out from under the flap of her rucksack. Abruptly, she stopped and turned to face him. 'Yeah? What you looking at?'

'Your magazine.' Henry wondered if she might let him borrow it when she'd finished.

'What about it?'

'Dottie told me about – about you wanting to be a pilot.'

She began to walk on. 'You can't believe everything Dottie tells you.' She looked at him defiantly. 'Only this time you can. Go on, say it! *Girls can't be pilots.* Well, they can, and I'm going to be one. I'm going to be in the RAF. When you see Tornados doing low-level flying stunts and zooming off to wars, that'll be me.'

'There might not be any wars,' Henry pointed out.

'Course there will! There's always a war on somewhere. If there isn't, somebody'll start one. That's just the way it is.'

'But why do you—'

'It's the Air Display on Saturday. Dad says I can go in the flight simulator,' Grace said importantly. 'I bet you'd like to go, wouldn't you, Strawberry Jam?'

'What Air Display?' Henry had never been to one. It sounded exciting, and just for a second he thought Grace was inviting him.

46

'Lakenfield,' she told him. 'Haven't you seen the posters? Must've been walking round with your eyes shut. Or are you too close to the ground to notice them? Me and Dad's going, just the two of us. Mum would have gone, but now there's Aunt Dottie.' She kicked at a stone.

'I like Aunt Dottie,' Henry said.

'Yeah, well. You know what?' She looked at Henry and smiled pleasantly. 'She's going to die. Only don't tell Mum I told you, right?'

Henry was too shocked to reply. Grace whistled a tune as she pushed open the gate to Number One.

Just as before, Pat and Dottie were in the back garden, with the Scrabble board on a low table.

'Hello, you two. Had a good day?' Pat asked, as if they were the best of friends.

'Yes, thanks,' Henry said, while Grace just shrugged.

'What was it like, then – did you feel like a very small fish in a very big pond?' Dottie asked. 'I remember what *that* feels like. Course, I never did get very big. Not like you will. They used to call me Pipsqueak when I was at school.'

'Mm,' was all Henry could say. He *had* felt like a little fish, trying to keep to the shallows, to avoid being gobbled up. But after what Grace had said, he could only look at Dottie with a sort of fascinated horror, as if she might go transparent, then slowly fade away altogether. Grace must have made it up! People who were about to die didn't sit in gardens playing Scrabble, looking perfectly cheerful. Reproachfully, he looked round at Grace, but she'd already gone indoors.

'Now, where were we?' Pat said, looking at the Scrabble board. 'Or p'raps we should start again and Henry can play?'

'Oh! Just seen something!' With thin hands, Dottie picked the ivory-coloured tiles off the rack in front of her, leaving only one behind. With an air of triumph, she placed them on the board so that her word finished with a Y that was already there. 'Good one!' She smiled mischievously. 'Look, Pat. That's 4-5-6-7-11-12-16 – and a double word score as well. 32 altogether! Not bad, eh?'

Henry knew the rules of Scrabble; they played it sometimes at Nan and Grandad's, at Christmas. Moving closer to look at the word Dottie had made, he read FIREFLY.

He stared, remembering the dancing specks of light by the orchard gate.

'I saw some of those,' he said. 'Fireflies. The other night.'

Dottie turned stiffly in her seat to look at him. Her blue eyes were round and surprised. 'Did you really? I used to see them, years and years ago, when I first lived here. But I haven't seen them for ages now. Glow-worms, they are, really. You don't get real fireflies, not in this country.'

Henry noticed that she was looking past him, towards the orchard, towards the gate. *She knows,* he thought. *I didn't say anything about* where *I saw them. She's looking at the exact place.* And he felt the prickling of goose-bumps at the back of his neck.

That man – Henry knew by now that he didn't live in the row of cottages. The people in Number Two were away on holiday, and Number Four belonged to an elderly couple. Perhaps it had been Jim Jessop, looking for his father's cat? But no, the smoking man hadn't been calling; and no one would come in search of a lost cat a whole year after it went missing. He was on the point of asking Dottie if she'd seen the man lurking, when she beckoned him to move the spare chair closer to hers. 'Come on, come and give me a hand. You'll be good at this, I bet,' she said. 'I don't want to start again, now I'm doing so well.'

'That puts you in the lead,' Pat said, writing down the new score. 'Take your letters, Dottie.' She held out the bag of tiles and Dottie dipped in and picked out six, to go with the one she had left.

Henry looked as she moved the seven letters around, forming bits of possible words.

'I can see one!'

'Go on, then. Show me,' Dottie said.

Henry slid three spare tiles to one end, out of the way, and rearranged the others to spell GATE.

Dottie nodded. 'That's good, Henry! We'd get an even better score with this, though.' *We.* They were a team now, Dottie and Henry. She picked up two more tiles, and moved them to spell GRATES.

But somehow the letters wanted to spell GATE. Dottie accidentally jolted the rack with her hand, and the R and the S fell off, landing on their faces on the white plastic table and skittering on to the lawn underneath. 'Oh, dear,' said Dottie. 'What a clumsy ha'porth! All fingers and thumbs, I am!'

Where had he heard that before? Something flitted into his mind, almost letting itself be caught before darting out of reach. Henry got down on his hands and knees to pick up the spilled letters, coming face to face with the word that remained: G ATE.

Dottie moved the tiles one at a time to the board. 'Firefly. Gate,' she said. Then she rummaged around in the bag of tiles. 'What's coming out next, I wonder?'

She looked at Henry. He felt that they shared a

secret, if only he knew what it was. When she picked out her new letters and turned the rack to show him, they spelled ESMIROP, nothing that made any sense at all.

SEVEN

Waiting

When Henry went back home with Dad at six o'clock, the cat was waiting outside on the kitchen window-sill, pressing itself against the glass. Dad opened the back door and it came in with a purring rush, heading straight up to Henry's room.

Henry followed him, calling *'Puss-Puss-Pudding!'* just the way Pat had said Mr Jessop used to call. Already up on the bed and deciding where to settle, the cat paused to gaze at him, perfectly still, eyes and ears alert. *'Puss-Puss-Pudding?'* Henry called again, more softly. The cat gave a tiny miaow in answer.

'You *are* Pudding, aren't you?' Henry felt quite sure. 'You know your name!'

The cat butted its head into his hand, wanting to be stroked. He petted it for a bit, then – reluctantly –

went downstairs to explain to Dad. Dad said that Pat ought to come round to check that it *was* Pudding, so that Jim Jessop could come and collect him.

'Oh yes, that's Pudding all right,' Pat said, a few minutes later. Pudding was by now curled up on Henry's bed, with no intention of moving, and only opened one eye when he heard the voices. 'You know, I clean forgot to phone Jim, but I'll go straight home and see if he'll come and fetch him. P'raps you'd better keep Pudding shut indoors – we don't want him disappearing again.'

Henry stayed with Pudding, sadly stroking his black fur, thinking how he would miss the warm purring presence in his room. Later, just after Mum got in from work, Pat came back. Henry heard the three of them talking downstairs.

'Well, I spoke to Jim—' (Pat had a clear, carrying voice) '—and he was pleased the cat's turned up, but it's a bit of a problem. They've recently got themselves a dog, see – a rescue case, very nervy and temperamental, and Pudding hates dogs. Looks like poor old Pudding'll have to go to the RSPCA, unless—'

Henry was already bounding down. 'We could keep him – can we?' he pleaded, looking from Mum to Dad and back again. 'He lives here! This is his home!'

Dad looked persuadable; Mum shook her head. 'I don't know. I've never had a cat – there'll be hairs on the furniture and scratches on the woodwork. And we can't leave him indoors when we're all out.'

'I could fit a cat-flap,' said Dad. Henry had never felt more grateful for Dad's new enthusiasm for DIY. 'In the back door, so he can come and go as he pleases. And it wouldn't be like having a kitten, that'd scratch and claw. Pudding's already settled here.'

'We-e-ll,' went Mum, in the tone of voice that meant she'd more or less given in. 'You'll have to look after him, Henry—'

'Great!' Henry raced upstairs, two at a time, to tell Pudding the good news. 'You're *ours* now, Pudding-Cat!' The cat looked at him through slits of eyes before curling himself more tightly to sleep. 'We'll get tins of cat food tomorrow,' Henry went on. 'And we'll buy you a collar and name-tag, in case you wander off again.'

Pudding showed no sign of wandering anywhere; he stayed on Henry's duvet all evening and was still sleeping there when Henry went up at bedtime.

'He's not to stay on your bed all night, Hen,' Mum called up the stairs. 'I've found him a box and put an old blanket in it. Bring him down before you turn your light off.'

'OK!' Henry called back, reluctant to disturb the cat; but, abruptly, Pudding was awake, staring towards the window. In three bounds he was off the bed and up on the sill; then he crouched, still as a cat-statue, eyes and ears focused on something outside.

Henry felt a tingling at the back of his neck. In the second before he went to the window and looked out at the dusk-shadowed orchard, he knew the strange man was back. And there he was, just as before: standing in the gateway, jacket over one shoulder, a cigarette raised to his lips. Henry saw the smouldering tip, and then, his eyes adjusting, the dance of the fireflies – glow-worms, Dottie had said, but he preferred to think of them as fireflies – flitting around the man's head like tiny points of light.

Henry opened the window wider and leaned out. 'Hey!' he shouted.

The man turned his head and looked in Henry's direction. Hardly breathing, Henry tried to memorise his appearance as best he could in the dim light: a smooth young face, hair cut short and neat, slim shoulders. Breathing out smoke that veiled his face, the man moved behind the hawthorn bush that grew beside the gate.

Henry wasn't going to let him slip out of sight.

He hurried downstairs, quietly as he could; Mum and Dad were watching TV in the front room and didn't hear him. The back door had been left open to the evening air; he paused there, seeing nothing, then darted out along the newly cleared flagstone path.

Surprised by his own daring, he pushed through the gate – it hadn't been used for some time and was snagged up with long grass.

No one there.

Henry looked around – at the stile on the farther side of the orchard and the footpath that ran diagonally across the next field; at the way back to the village, past Pat's house, to where the path came out opposite the church. No sign of anyone. The grass wasn't even flattened.

But he could smell cigarette smoke. He stood there, breathing it in, and that strange feeling came back to him – the sense of being in someone else's body. He felt the starched shirt collar stiff round his neck, his feet hot in wool socks, and a sore place on one heel where his boot had rubbed; he felt the flat weight of his cigarette lighter in his jacket pocket. He heard a girl's voice humming, heard the creak of the Rectory gate as it was pushed open and felt a leap of joy as she came towards him through the trees. She wore the sky-blue dress he liked best, with the neat round collar, and her hair was clipped to one side, falling in soft waves.

'You do like to keep me waiting!' he called to her.

'Sorry!' She ducked beneath a low branch, then stopped, keeping a few yards between them. 'But I can't come yet – not yet. You'll wait, won't you?' Then she stepped back, staring at his face. 'Oh! I thought you were Henry, but—'

'Course I'm Henry! Who are you?'

'What do you mean, who am I?'

He blinked and his eyes blurred, then cleared.

'Durr-brain, Strawberry Pip! Why're you pretending you don't know me?' the girl's voice said, sharp and loud.

Grace, unmistakably Grace, in shorts and trainers and a loose T-shirt. He blinked and shook his head – he must have dreamed the sky-blue dress, the wavy hair. She had scrambled up into one of the apple trees, clinging high, both feet on a low branch; she bounced on it, as if testing whether she could snap the wood with her weight. 'You mental or something? Isn't it past your bedtime – you sleepwalking or what?'

'Well, what are you doing?' he retorted, so confused that he wasn't sure whether he'd sleepwalked out here or not.

'Climbed out the bathroom window,' Grace said. She chose a different branch, hooked both legs over and swung upside down, her arms brushing the grass. 'I do that when I feel like it. Course, I could just walk out the door, but climbing down the drainpipe's much more fun.'

'Did you see—'

'Did I see what, Strawberry Pip?'

'Did you see anyone else out here? A man with a cigarette? And a girl – older than you, in a blue dress – coming through the trees?'

Grace unhooked her legs from the tree and did a handstand on the grass, then flipped over and sprang to her feet. 'No, didn't see anyone. Just you, standing in the dark mumbling to yourself.'

Henry breathed in slowly, closing his eyes. 'Can you smell cigarette smoke?'

She sniffed, this way and that, wrinkling her nose like a rabbit. 'No.' Then she punched his arm in delight. 'What, you sneaked out for a secret fag, Midget? Is that what you're up to?'

'Puh!' Henry retorted. 'Why'd I want to fill my lungs with tar? And even if I was stupid enough, why'd I stand right here where anyone can see me from indoors?'

But there was no stopping Grace in this kind of mood. 'Ooh, what a little rebel! Mummy and

Daddy won't half be cross if they find out what their little Strawberry Squidge is up to! Better make sure they don't, hadn't you?'

Henry had had enough of Grace. 'See you to-morrow. If I have to,' he flung at her, and stomped through the gate, dragging it shut behind him.

'I thought you'd gone up to bed!' Mum said, indoors. 'And was that Grace I saw you talking to? Told you you'd soon be friends, didn't I?'

EIGHT

Amber

By the end of the second day at Hartsfield High, Henry felt much less conspicuous and new – especially as the weather was so hot that not a single sweatshirt was in sight, red, green or any other colour, so he didn't stand out. He was almost sorry that he wouldn't be at school with Simon and the others for the last week of term. But Simon was coming round on Sunday – it had been Mum's idea for Henry to invite him – so there was now someone he could call a friend.

On the coach home, the talk was of the Air Display next day at Lakenfield; Jonathan, Neil and Elissa were all going, with their families. Simon pulled a face and said that he had to go to a wedding, a friend of his mother's he hardly knew.

'Boring! I'd much rather go to Lakenfield. You going?' he asked Henry.

Henry said he would ask Dad, but suspected that there'd still be too much house stuff going on.

Simon's mother was waiting for him, as before, parked outside the village shop. As he ran across the green he called back to Henry, 'See you Sunday!'

'Come on,' Grace said impatiently, as if Henry were a dog that hadn't yet learned to follow at heel. Henry thought he might just dump his bag at Pat's, then come back out to see if any of the other boys were playing football in the rec. But Grace had other ideas.

While Pat and Dottie asked Henry about his day, she changed into jeans, made herself a peanut butter sandwich, gulped down some lemonade and told Pat, 'I'm going to see Amber.'

'No, you're not,' Pat said. 'I've told you before, you're not walking across the fields by yourself. You'll have to wait till Tracy can go with you.'

'She's at the dentist,' Grace said sulkily. Then she brightened. 'I know! Henry can come.'

'Who's Amber?' Henry asked.

'A pony I ride sometimes. It's not far. You can have a ride if you like.'

Henry knew she was only offering because she

wouldn't be allowed to go otherwise, but he said, 'OK, then.'

He and Grace walked across the field behind the church, Grace still eating her sandwich. It was a hot, drowsy afternoon, with midges in clouds beneath the trees by the stream. The grass had been cut for hay, and the stalks crunched stiffly under Henry's trainers as he walked. He wondered why Pat wouldn't let Grace come out here on her own – Crickford St. Thomas was such a quiet place, not like London, where Mum and Dad had always been warning him about being careful and not going off with anyone or getting into strange cars. As if he would! Here, the only lurking stranger was the man at the firefly gate, and he never seemed to appear in daylight.

The path across the hayfield led to a stony track. Her sandwich finished, Grace picked up a twig and thwacked it at the flowering grasses and nettles by the ditch, humming a tune Henry recognised. Then, looking at him, she started singing the words.

'He landed on the runway like a dollop of strawberry jam . . . Do you know that song, Strawberry?'

'The tune,' Henry said. 'Not the words.' Was she going to keep going on about strawberries for ever and ever? Strawberry, Pick-Your-Own, Milkshake,

Squidge: she and her friend Tracy seemed to find endless amusement in thinking up new variations. It annoyed Henry that he minded. Why should he?

'It's your song, Squidge,' Grace said, giggling. 'It's an old RAF song. D'you know how it starts?'

'No, I just told you. I don't know it.'

'It goes like this.' Grace stopped walking and faced Henry squarely. *'He jumped without a parachute from forty thousand feet . . .'* She frowned. 'Actually I got it wrong just now. It goes: *They scraped him off the runway like a dollop of strawberry jam . . .'*

'So what?' Henry said. He didn't know how she expected him to react, but to his annoyance he felt his face flushing, hot red like a ripe strawberry.

'I'm going back,' he told Grace, 'if you're going to keep going on at me. Didn't have to come, did I? And you won't be able to ride your stupid pony if I don't come. So shut up about strawberries.'

Grace looked down, scuffing her shoe on the gravelly path. 'If you don't come with me I'll tell your Mum and Dad you were smoking.'

'Go ahead,' Henry said, pretending to turn back. 'I wasn't, and they'll believe me, not you.'

'OK, don't get in a strop!' Grace called after him. 'Come with me and I'll stop calling you names – promise. But Amber's not stupid.'

'Well, *you* are. Anyway,' Henry said nastily, just to make sure he had the last word, 'you're the one who wants to be a pilot. You might be the one who crashes on a runway. If you ever get as far as being a pilot, that is. Your mum says you'll be too tall.'

Grace gave him a snooty sideways look. 'That's what *she* says. That's cos she doesn't think I can really do it. But tall people *can* be fighter pilots – I've found out. So don't start talking as if you know more than me, Midget, cos you don't.'

'Still,' Henry persevered, 'just *anyone* can't do it. You have to pass loads of selection tests first and it's really hard.'

'I know that! I'm going to pass them all. And I'm not going to crash. I'm going to be the best pilot ever. You don't believe me, do you? Girls can do anything better than boys.'

She whistled a snatch of her strawberry song in an absent-minded way, though Henry knew she was doing it on purpose. Then, not looking to see if he was coming, she broke into a jog-trot across the next field. Henry knew that if he ran too, she'd run even faster; he was a good runner, but she had much longer legs and would easily beat him. For a few seconds he considered going home after all, but by now he was curious to see the pony, so carried on walking at his own pace.

At the end of the next field, Grace sat on a five-bar gate, swinging her legs. 'Come on, snail. What kept you?' She turned and pointed to a fence with a gate beneath a tall tree. 'That's Amber's field.'

Amber was a fat sleek pony, cream-gold, with a black mane and tail. She was dozing under a tree as they approached, but whinnied and came trotting when she saw Grace. There was a small wooden shelter by the gate, which Grace unlocked with a key she took out of her jeans pocket. Inside there was a saddle and bridle, brushes and buckets and a bin of horse feed. The pony pushed against the gate, eager for the sugar lumps Grace held out flat on her palm. She was bigger than Henry had expected, almost a horse.

'Is she yours?' Henry asked.

Grace snorted, like a pony herself. 'Course not. I can't afford a pony. But I'm allowed to ride her. She belongs to the lady in the house over there but she's out at work most of the time and only rides at weekends. You can help me brush her if you like.'

Henry picked up a brush and started to groom Amber, so delicately that she swished her tail as if he were an annoying fly.

'Not like that – like this,' Grace bossed. 'Brush hard. You don't have to be scared. She won't bite.'

'I'm not scared,' Henry said. He liked the look of Amber. Her coat was beautifully shiny and her eyes were big and dark brown, with long eyelashes. Her body was as round as a barrel but her legs were slim, with small neat hooves. While Henry brushed her, she turned her neck and touched him softly with her nose. He didn't need Grace to tell him she wouldn't bite. It was obvious she was a gentle pony.

Grace put the bridle on and fastened the straps. 'I'll ride first, then you can have a go. We'll ride bareback, it's more fun.'

She vaulted astride, then gathered the reins and clicked with her tongue. Henry watched as she rode round the field a few times. It didn't look very difficult; the pony looked calm and well behaved, not likely to rear up or bolt or do anything dramatic. But Henry felt a bit nervous about trying in front of Grace; she'd make fun of him as soon as he did something wrong.

Grace cantered all the way from the end of the field, then pulled up and slid off. 'Your go now.'

As Henry wasn't tall enough to vault on the way she had, she gave him a leg-up, nearly pitching him right over the pony and off the other side. Amber's sides were warm and smooth, but there was nothing to hang on to and the reins got themselves into a tangle. He would have felt safer with a saddle and stirrups.

'Here, like this.' Grace sorted out the reins for him. 'I'll lead you first, then you can try on your own.'

Walking wasn't too bad, though Henry felt very high up and tried not to look down at the grass or imagine falling off. *They scraped him off the runway like a dollop of strawberry jam* . . . The words of Grace's stupid song kept going through his mind. But there was no runway, only soft grass; anyway, he needn't fall off if he concentrated. Then Grace made her tongue-clicking sound to make the pony trot, with Henry bouncing almost uncontrollably, only a handful of mane keeping him on Amber's back. They kept up this uncomfortable pace to the farthest corner of the field, till both Grace and Henry were puffed out. Soon, he thought, it would be over, and his feet would be safely back on the ground.

But Grace hadn't finished yet. 'Now you can try a canter,' she said. 'It's easy. Just hang on. She'll stop at the gate.'

'No! I—'

Grace wasn't listening. She picked a twiggy stick out of the hedge, let go of Amber's reins, waved the stick wildly and yelled, 'Go, Amber!'

The pony leaped forward. Henry's head jerked back and his legs shot out, but somehow he was still on, lurching forward to grab a handful of Amber's thick mane. He was losing his balance, slipping off to one side and then the other, looking down at the pony's hooves that pounded the grass. In a moment he would be down there, trampled. Panic clutched at him. The reins had slipped from his hands and he had no way to steer or make the pony stop. He heard Grace shrieking, 'Go, Amber!' and was suddenly determined not to fall off – that was obviously what Grace wanted. He found the strength to grip with his legs, grabbed Amber's mane with both hands and, for a few seconds, felt in control of himself, rocking with the movement. The gate loomed and he hoped the pony wouldn't try to jump – it looked terrifyingly high and solid. Then she swerved, almost throwing him off to one side, and came to a juddering halt, flinging up her head and nearly hitting him on the nose.

Suddenly he was aware of the silence of the after-noon meadow, the bees drowsing in the hedge, a brown speckled butterfly settling on a bramble flower, as if the drama of the last few minutes hadn't happened at all. His heart was pounding and his legs shaking, but he was still on the pony's back.

He'd show that stupid girl!

He disentangled the reins, then turned the pony's head and clucked with his tongue the way Grace did. Obediently, Amber started to walk away from the gate, towards Grace, who was half running across the field.

She was laughing, doubling up as if she had a bad stitch. 'You did look funny, Strawberry Pip! Hanging round her neck like a monkey up a stick. I thought you'd end up in a pile of dung. Wait till I tell Tracy!'

Henry wasn't going to let her know how terrified he'd been or that he knew what she'd tried to do.

'It was all right,' he said coolly. 'Once I got the hang of it.'

Grace giggled. 'Next time, I'll put up some jumps,' she said. 'If you think you're so good.'

Henry slithered to the ground, landing on wavery legs that only just held him up. Next time. There was going to be a next time. And Henry knew he'd have to come or Grace would think he'd chickened out. He'd managed to conceal his fear this time, but he'd have to do it again, and Grace would make it harder every time.

They scraped him off the runway like a dollop of strawberry jam . . .

NINE

Fly Past

Each day, during the hours of sunlight, Henry found it quite impossible to believe that he'd ever really seen the smoking man by the gate, and the fireflies. The sense of being inside someone else's body – in someone else's clothes and shoes – had been so strong that he must surely have dreamed it. Only when dusk fell over the fields and woods, and he was alone in his bedroom or with only Pudding for company, did he start to feel edgy and anxious. Every few minutes he had to go to the window, to check there was no one by the orchard gate.

Already, though it was nowhere near dark, something was pulling him to the window. Everything looked normal. The lightest of breezes ruffled the long grasses in the orchard, stirring the leaves of the apple trees; a wood pigeon cooed from the roof above him; he heard a train, a long way distant. No one was out there; he was quite sure of that. Then, looking to his left, he caught his breath as he saw someone farther along, by the gate of Number One. Dottie. Only Dottie, steadying herself with a hand on the fence. But she was looking intently towards Henry's gate, towards the place where the young man had stood.

Maybe she'd seen him too! Why hadn't he thought of asking? Henry ran downstairs – almost tripping over Pudding, who had decided to curl up and sleep two steps down from the landing – and let himself out into the garden. He pushed open the gate to the orchard, noticing that the grass was now flattened where he'd trodden on it last night. He was about to call out to Dottie when he saw that she had turned and was going back towards the house. Voices floated out into the garden, Grace's and Pat's, arguing.

Henry couldn't help creeping closer along the orchard fence to hear what the fuss was about. A few moments later he wished he hadn't – they were talking about *him*.

'No, I don't *want* him to come!' That was Grace; he could imagine the sulky face, the defiant posture. 'I have to put up with him every day after

71

school, don't I – can't I have a day out for once, just Dad and me on our own?'

'Oh, come on, Grace.' Pat. 'Try to think of someone else, for a change. Henry's just moved here, he hardly knows anyone, I'm sure he'd like to go—'

'Henry? The Air Display? Oh, I bet he'd love it.' That was Dottie's warm voice with the chuckle in it. 'You could have a lovely day, the two of you and your Dad—'

'No! I want to go with Dad, just the two of us! I don't want to be lumbered with a little kid like Henry. It'll all be ruined if he tags along!'

'Don't be so obstinate,' Pat tried. 'Why should it be spoiled?'

'Because it will! If you're so keen for Henry to go, tell you what, Henry can go with Dad and I'll stay at home.'

There was a silence then. Maybe Grace had stomped into another room or gone all huffy and refused to say any more. Afraid of someone coming out into the garden and seeing him sneak away, Henry crept back to his own gate. He felt hot all over with embarrassment and the sense of unfairness. *A little kid like Henry* – the cheek of Grace! After he'd trudged over the fields with her this afternoon, so that she could ride Amber! It must have been Pat's idea for him to go to the Air

Display; he hadn't invited himself, had he? He wanted to go, really wanted, after hearing Simon and the others talk about it; but he knew that Mum and Dad would have to stay in tomorrow, because an electrician was coming and someone to fit carpet.

Anyway, he thought with a rush of defiance, I'd rather miss it than go with that nasty, spiteful *user*.

As it turned out, a lot of the Air Display came over the cottage, so Henry didn't miss it after all. He was helping Dad to clear the garden, sorting out broken flower-pots and bits of glass and tangles of ivy and cobwebs, when the Red Arrows zoomed overhead. They flew over with a tearing swoosh, so low that Henry couldn't help ducking; then they fanned out as if unzipping the sky into three sections.

No more garden clearing took place after that. Henry and Dad stood by the back gate, peering into the sky, waiting to see what would happen next.

'We'll definitely go next year,' Dad said. 'But it looks as if we'll get quite a good view from here.'

Mum came out, bringing the binoculars, and they took turns at squinting into the sky and trying to focus. 'Our own private air-show!' Mum said. 'No need to queue in traffic or search for parking places or toilets. And it's free!'

Later, when they heard the jangle of an ice-cream

van outside, Dad bought choc ices, so that they really could pretend they were having a day out. Getting neck ache from craning upwards, they watched helicopters, a pair of stunt biplanes with people standing on the wings, then fighters with an ear-numbing thunderclap of jet engines. Next – getting a cheer from Dad – Spitfires and a Lancaster, two small planes and a large one with a blunt nose.

'Old war planes,' he explained. 'Grandad worked on Spitfires in the war, as an engineer. Here, have a good look.'

Henry adjusted the binoculars and saw the two small planes like clockwork toys flanking the bigger Lancaster. The drone of their engines, he thought, was even more exciting than the great whoosh of the jets that had flown over earlier. The din of the supercharged jets had made the whole sky shake, but the sound of these engines – old wartime engines – was somehow more thrilling. It made the planes seem brave and determined, pushing against the sky.

'There were lots of airfields round here in the war,' Dad said. 'Because it's so flat, and so near the coast. Lakenfield was one. Grandad worked at Waddington, up near Lincoln.'

He had once shown Henry a photo of his grandfather – Henry's great-grandfather – as a young mechanic in overalls, winding up the propeller of a Spitfire. In the cockpit sat a faceless figure in goggles, muffled up in a scarf. How odd that a fighter pilot was what Grace wanted to be! In his imagination, he substituted her for the goggled pilot in the photograph. She looked ludicrous. Girls might be able to train as fighter pilots now, but they certainly hadn't fought in combat in the Second World War. Henry knew that much.

'Afternoon, Dottie!' Dad suddenly called out, above the retreating drone of the aircraft as they flew into the sun. 'Enjoying the show?'

Henry looked along in the direction of Pat's garden. Dottie was by the washing spinner, holding it with one hand to steady herself. She held up the other hand to shield her eyes as she gazed towards the aircraft being swallowed up by the sun's glare. She didn't hear Dad at first; after a few moments she turned, blinking and confused, like someone waking up slowly. Then Pat came out of the house and called to Dad across Number Two's garden: 'Come and have a cup of tea. I bet you could do with a break.'

Dad explained about the electrician and the carpet fitter, but Pat told him to leave a note on the front door saying *Please knock at Number One*, and they all went along – Mum, Dad and Henry. It was much nicer, Henry thought, going to Pat's when Grace wasn't there.

'Wotcha, Henry,' Dottie said, giving him a huge wink. 'We get just as good a view from here, don't we?'

Henry kept thinking about what Grace had said, that Dottie was going to die. She might be making it up – you couldn't tell, with Grace. But if it was true, what did it mean? Would Dottie carry on getting thinner and thinner and smaller and smaller? Would she be taken away to hospital? Or would she simply not be there one day? But whenever Dottie spoke to him and looked at him with those amazingly bright blue eyes, she seemed far too full of life to be at any risk of dying.

'Takes me right back, seeing them planes,' she said, as Mum and Dad sat down. 'That was the Battle of Britain Memorial Flight, did you know that? That Lancaster's one of only two in the world that can still fly. The other one's over in Canada or somewhere. Apart from that, you only see them in museums.' She sighed. 'Think of all that effort, making them. They used to fly right over here, them Lancasters, three or four times a week. I used to count them out as they flew off towards the sea, and count them safely in when they came back. Enormous, a Lanc seemed then. Course, if you saw one now, next to one of them big Jumbos, it'd look like nothing at all.'

'You were here in the war?' Dad asked.

Dottie nodded, holding out her cup to Pat for a refill of tea. 'That's right, love.'

Henry thought it was funny the way she called Dad 'Love', as if she thought of him as just a boy.

'Evacuated from the East End, I was,' she went on. 'Me and my sister. Came to live at the Old Rectory just behind the church.' She nodded in the direction she meant. 'You know the house with the big lime trees? Fell on our feet, we did. Not like some. They treated us like family at the Rectory. Even though they was so posh, and us just a couple of scruffy Bethnal Green kids.'

'So you never went back to London?' Mum asked.

Dottie shook her head. 'Betty married and settled in Ipswich. I was going to get married too, only it never came off. But I liked it here in Suffolk, so I stayed. I worked in the NAAFI canteen for a bit, then later I got a job in the aircraft factory. After the war I learned to type and got an office job. Me, I never did get married, but I got a job in Ipswich, to be near Betty. She was the only family I had after Mum and Dad died.'

Henry twiddled a stalk of grass, sitting by Dad's

feet with a glass of Coke. He couldn't imagine someone as old as Dottie having a Mum and Dad. Or making aircraft in a factory. He'd seen pictures – rows of girls and women working away, wearing overalls and turbans, singing while they worked to make the hours pass. Making bits of Spitfires and Hurricanes.

'You know what?' he said to Dottie. 'You could have made a bit for one of those Spitfires that just went over!'

Dottie smiled at him. 'Maybe I did, Henry love. Who knows?' And she gazed into the sky where the planes had been. 'Just seventeen, I was, when I moved out here. East End girl straight from the Blitz. Glad to get grass under my feet instead of pavement.' Then she looked at Henry in an odd way, that made him think it was someone else she was seeing, not him at all. She went on, 'We hadn't been here long when I met him, on the airfield.'

'Met him?' Mum asked. 'Who?'

'Henry,' Dottie said. For a second she sounded like Grace – impatient, answering in a *who-did-you-think-I-meant* sort of way. *Who did you think I was talking about?* Henry stared at her, and Mum echoed, 'You met Henry?'

'Yes, he—' Dottie began. But at that point another aircraft came over, drowning what she said, and they all looked up at what Dad said was a Hercules, a huge, bulky plane that looked too heavy to get off the ground. Then, when the noise faded, there was a loud ring at the front door followed by an impatient rapping – someone had obviously been waiting to be heard for a while. It was the electrician and the carpet man, both at once.

Later, when the new carpet had been laid in the front room and the air was full of tiny fibres that got into his nose and tickled, Henry went outside in case any last aircraft displays or parachute jumps could be seen. Mum and Dad were making sandwiches for tea in the kitchen.

'Do you think she's a bit gaga? Dottie, I mean?' Mum asked. She was speaking in a low voice, but Henry could still hear.

'Talking about Henry, you mean?' Dad said. 'I shouldn't think so – she's sharp enough otherwise. But she does seem to have taken quite a liking to him.'

Dottie, gaga! Henry wanted to rush in and shout at Mum, 'Of course she isn't! She's as clever as you are, and much better at Scrabble!'

Gaga!

But he didn't go in. It would be difficult to explain why he liked Dottie so much – more than anyone else he'd met since moving to Crickford St.

Thomas. He looked across at Pat's garden, but they'd all gone indoors, taking the chairs and the Scrabble with them – there were only a few starlings on the lawn, pecking at cake crumbs. He felt cleverer than Mum and Dad: obviously Dottie hadn't meant him. There was another Henry.

He would ask her on Monday.

TEN

Counting them Out, Counting them Back In

Sunday afternoon was so hot that when Henry stepped outside it felt as if the sun was melting him into gloopiness, like a wax candle. Even Mum and Dad tired of gardening and sat reading the Sunday papers in the shade outside the back door. Henry had thought he and Simon might play football at the rec, but it was far too hot for that.

'We could go over to the stream,' Simon suggested. 'There might be sticklebacks.'

'Can we?' Henry asked his parents. He knew by now that Simon liked wildlife of all sorts, particularly frogs and toads.

'How far is it?' Mum asked Simon.

Simon made a vague guesture. 'Not far. That way, out in the fields. There's a footpath.'

Once Mum had satisfied herself that they wouldn't have to trespass or cross any fields with bulls in them, she agreed. 'Don't get too hot,' she warned.

It would be impossible *not* to get too hot, Henry thought, unless you stood up to your neck in a river. He felt the sun striking through his T-shirt and prickling his bare arms as Simon led the way along the footpath beside the church and out into a grass meadow.

'I've been this way before,' he told Simon, recognising the way Grace had brought him on Friday. The stream – the tree-shaded part of it Simon was making for – was down in the dip to their left; ahead, over the brow of a rise, was the stony track that led towards Amber's paddock. It would be fun, Henry thought, to show Amber to Simon, and impress him with the story of the wild gallop. He'd call Amber a horse, he decided, rather than a pony; she was almost big enough to pass for a horse. He could make it sound like a one-horse Grand National. 'Let's go this way first,' he told Simon.

A flurry of birds flew out from the low trees beside the stream and the water glinted coolly, making him wonder for a moment if it wouldn't be more fun after all to paddle and look for stickle-backs. They reached the stile that led to the stony track, which they followed until it forked by a barn. Here, Henry soon realised that he must have taken a wrong turning. There was no shelter, no pony. Instead the field-edge was rising slowly towards a rusted gate. The rough path under their feet ran beside a dry ditch fringed with poppies and nettles, then became concrete, cracked and broken, with grass pushing up through the cracks. Henry and Simon climbed the gate and stood looking at the flat, open area, bordered by shrubby trees. The track widened, joining another at a sharp angle.

'You know what this place is?' Simon whispered.

Henry had no idea why Simon felt he had to keep his voice low – there was no one around – but he found himself whispering too. 'No. What?'

'It's the old airfield. This is one of the runways. And that building over there must have been some sort of control tower.'

Henry looked at the crumbling brick building with broken steps leading up to a doorway. 'How old?' he asked. 'This place doesn't look as if it's been used for centuries.'

'There weren't such things as aeroplanes centuries ago, dingbat.' Simon gave him a friendly shove.

'It was used in the war. I know cos my Grandad was here, Grandad Dobbs.'

'What did he do in the war, your grandad?'

'Actually he's my Great-grandad – my Dad's Grandad. He's ancient, eighty-something. He flew in a Lancaster. But he wasn't a pilot, he was a flight engineer. He told me all about it. There were seven of them, in a Lanc, all with different jobs: pilot, wireless operator, rear gunner – I forget the others. And all Grandad's crew were killed one night, only Grandad wasn't there cos he was in sick bay, with flu. They all died, all his best mates he'd been with since he trained. For a long time, he said, he wished he'd died with them. He felt guilty, for getting flu. He should have been there.'

'To get killed? That's a weird thing to wish.'

Simon shrugged. 'That's what he said.'

'So didn't he fly any more after that?'

'Course he did! The war was still on. But he got transferred to some other airfield, with another crew. He was lucky, he said. One time he was due to fly, only there was something wrong with their plane so they couldn't go, and seven out of the twenty planes got shot down that night. And another time he'd just left his position to go for a pee – they had this chemical toilet thing in the back, he said, it stank something awful – when a stream of bullets from a fighter tore through the fuselage right where he'd been sitting. That's how he got his nickname. Lucky Dobbs. Before, he was always called Rusty.'

'Rusty? Dobbs?' Henry's mind snagged on the names. For a second he felt his feet hot in boots and smelled crushed grass and doughnuts. Next moment that thought had flittered just out of reach, like a piece of thistledown on the wind. If only he could catch and hold it . . .

'Yeah, Rusty, cos he had red hair just like me,' Simon explained. 'But after all these lucky misses, it was Lucky Dobbs. His crew started to think he was their good luck mascot. He could fall in a dung heap and come up smelling of roses, they said.'

Got it! Into Henry's mind floated the grinning face from his dream, the bright eyes. Rusty Dobbs! But how – As soon as he'd grasped it, tried to make sense of it, he began to doubt his memory. Perhaps he hadn't dreamed the name Rusty Dobbs at all – had only heard it a few moments ago from Simon. Then another thought struck him. 'You know what? The first time, when he had flu – if it wasn't for those flu germs, you wouldn't be here now.'

'I know.'

'You owe that flu bug.'

'Thank you, O generous germs,' Simon said

solemnly, with a little bow. 'Or if he hadn't needed to pee.'

They walked on, along the cracked runway. The air rose from the baked concrete in a faint shimmer of heat. Something about the place made Henry feel edgy. The words of Grace's stupid song ran through his head again: *They scraped him off the runway like a dollop of strawberry jam* . . . He hated that song, without having the faintest idea why it should bother him so much. But, in the war, it must have been real. People must have had to parachute out of flaming planes, had to decide: jump, or die in your burning aircraft.

He almost reeled with dizziness, facing himself with that choice. Blackness took over his mind, unfathomable, streaked with flares and tracer fire and explosions. It took an effort to bring himself back to *now*, his feet solidly on the ground, walking over the concrete and the thrusting weeds. Another runway swept across the middle of the airfield between big triangles of grass that had been cut for hay. Any minute now, he thought, remembering what Mum had said about only walking on proper footpaths, a farmer would drive up on a tractor and tell them off for trespassing. It felt wrong to be here. All the same, he'd rather face the angry farmer than the fear that was making his stomach churn and his legs tremble.

An old hangar loomed at them behind a dense belt of shrubs. Henry had a wild vision of it being full of brand new Spitfires, straight from the factories. He imagined young pilots in overalls running towards them and leaping into the cockpits, the way he'd seen in the old films Dad liked to watch. He hesitated, but Simon walked straight up and looked in at the open front.

'Hay bales,' he said. He sounded disappointed, as if he'd had the same idea as Henry. 'The farmer's using it as a barn.'

Henry felt as if they'd walked right out of the real world. He wondered if they'd be able to find their way back to the village but, when he turned and looked, he could see the church tower of Crickford St. Thomas rising above the trees of the Old Rectory, less than a mile away.

'Come on!' Simon shouted. 'I'll be a Spitfire, you be a Stuka dive-bomber!' And he ran along the runway, arms out, making an 'Eeeee-ow!' noise as he swerved and ducked. Henry tried to make Stuka noises and actions, but it didn't feel right in this strange place. He fended off the Spitfire attacks half-heartedly, and was glad when Simon tired, wilting in the heat.

'Let's go down to your stream,' Henry said. 'Or I'll burst into flames.'

At home, tea was all cold things – ham and salad, strawberries with ice-cream, orange juice with chunks of ice. Henry told his parents about the deserted airfield, and after the meal Dad fetched the local map. Henry had the odd feeling that if he tried to return, he wouldn't find it.

'Yes, here it is.' Dad's finger pointed at the triangles of runway, not far from the orange lines of roads and grey rectangles of houses that marked the village. 'Airfield, disused. Risingheath.'

Simon leaned over to point. 'This green dotted line means public footpath – look, it leads there from behind the church, the way we went. So we weren't trespassing after all.'

'Risingheath. I remember the name now,' Dad said, peering closer. 'I read it in some war book or other. But you know who you could ask, if you want to know more?'

'My Grandad,' Simon said promptly. 'Great-grandad, really. He was there.'

'Was he really?' Dad said. 'I was going to say, ask Dottie. She was here in the war. She'd know about it. What did your Great-grandad do?'

Simon was telling the story of Rusty Dobbs's flu when his mother arrived to take him home.

Although it was nearly half-past nine, it still wasn't dark. Henry felt too wide-awake for sleep; the back door was open and he wandered out along the flagged path with a glass of milk in his hand, putting off bed-time. Mum and Dad had been working hard at the garden and it was gradually getting tidier. Where there had been tangles of bramble and teasel and nettles, there was now dug earth. A huge heap of dried plants waited near the back gate to be turned into compost, in the compost-bin Dad was going to make as his next project.

By the gate at the end of the garden, Henry stopped and looked out at the orchard, through the bent, twisted shapes of the apple trees. On such a warm night he expected to see the fireflies, their points of flame flickering and weaving. He'd almost told Simon about them, as Simon knew things about frogs and newts and sticklebacks and probably glow-worms as well; but had stopped on the verge of asking, suddenly sure that these glow-worms weren't for everyone to see.

There they were, flittering and dancing, just as he'd been sure they would be. But there was no shadowy figure standing at the gate this time, no twist of cigarette smoke. Just the fireflies, dancing for themselves.

Henry turned and looked towards Pat's house. One of the upstairs windows was lit – the window of the room that matched Henry's, jutting out at the back. He saw a thin, white-clad figure standing there, half hidden by the curtains, looking out. For a moment he thought it was Grace, but then he saw the gleam of light on grey hair and realised that it was Dottie. Henry waved, but she showed no sign of having seen him. She was gazing towards the firefly gate.

Dottie hadn't seen fireflies – glow-worms – for years, she'd told him. Well, she must be seeing them now. But there was something strange about the way she stood there without moving – just like Pudding when he fixed his eyes on some tiny movement that Henry couldn't even see.

'Henry! What you doing out there? It's past your bed-time!' Dad called from the back door. Henry drank the last of the milk and went in.

In the middle of the night, Henry woke up with a lurch, his heart thumping. Something was different.

Engines. He could hear engines and just for a second imagined he was back at home, hearing the roar of traffic that never stopped. But the engine noise was overhead; it thrummed and drummed at his ears, making him dizzy. Dozens of aircraft must be flying right overhead. Weird! A flight from Lakenfield, he thought; then realised that what he was hearing was propeller-driven aircraft, not the tearing sound jet engines would make. He got out of bed and went to the window.

A round disc of moon lit up slivers of cloud. Flying towards the moon, in silhouette, were aircraft in formation. Henry recognised the blunt noses, the cigar-shaped bodies and the flat tail-spars of Lancaster bombers. He wouldn't have known what they were until last Saturday, but now he was sure.

Lancaster bombers.

He must count them all out and he must count them back in.

Pudding was perched on the gate, a dark shape in the moonlight. He crouched, ears flat, then abruptly leaped down and streaked towards the back door. Henry heard the slap and swing of the cat-flap as he rocketed in.

I must keep counting, Henry thought. Ten, eleven, twelve, like a flock of wild geese, high and purposeful, flying out in the direction of Lowestoft and the sea. They shone silver in the moonlight. Twelve Lancaster bombers.

But that was impossible! Henry stood at the window and watched as the leaders were swallowed up in the bank of cloud. When they were all out of sight, he stared and stared at the grey fuzziness of cloud until his eyes went blurry.

Silence. He strained his ears into the night, but heard only the hoot of an owl. He had no idea what time it was, but the house felt still. When he stepped back from the window, the floorboards creaked with night-time eeriness. The back of his neck had gone all tingly and the skin on his arms was goose-bumped. He lurched for his bed, and clicked on the bed-side light. At once the room was lit up, warm and bright and normal, everything jumping out at him in sharp colours, apart from the slab of blackness at the window where he'd pushed back the curtain. He tugged the curtains closed, so that not an inch of darkness showed between them.

Then he lay down and listened to the words in his head.

It'll be thirteen next time.

Count them out and count them back in.

He wanted Pudding, wanted to cuddle him. No matter what Mum said about cats on beds, he wanted Pudding's warm purring company. He crept downstairs and opened the kitchen door. At once Pudding surged through and straight upstairs, his tail bristling like a toilet-brush.

'Come on, Pud. You can stay with me.' Henry picked up the struggling cat. 'P'raps I'm dreaming. P'raps we both are.'

At last the cat settled beside him. Hours later, from the depths of sleep, Henry found himself counting again: felt the windows shake to the roar of engines, felt their shadows low overhead. *One. Two, three. Four. Five, six, seven. Eight.*

Nine.

Nine.

Nine.

Nine.

Nine.

Twelve out and only nine back.

Your turn next.

Thirteen.

ELEVEN

Henry's Haunt

Monday, and Henry was almost wishing he could go to school with Simon and the others. It didn't feel like the summer holidays, not yet; not with everyone else still at school. When he'd been with Simon and the others, or with Mum and Dad, all the strangeness of dreams and coincidences seemed less important – just stray thoughts. When he was on his own, he couldn't stop thinking about them.

Where was it all going? Where was it taking him? What was it all *for?* Sometimes he wondered if he was seriously losing his marbles – he must be, if he couldn't even tell what was real and what wasn't.

There was a papery clatter of post through the letter-box. Going to pick it up, expecting the usual dull stuff for Mum and Dad, Henry's eyes went straight to a letter with his own name on it, and four Arsenal stickers. Nabil! Inside was a postcard of a brontosaurus and one of Nabil's cartoons. He'd drawn Henry up a haystack with a snorting bull at the bottom and himself perched on the very top of the London Eye, each looking at the other through a telescope. Nabil was good at cartoons. 'The dinosaur's from the Natural History Museum,' he had written on the back of the postcard. 'Dad's taking us there when you come – we thought it'd be nice for you to meet some relations. Hurry up and get your email sorted out!'

Henry felt cheered up by that, less anxious about being in the house by himself, even if Nabil was miles and miles away. Officially, Pat was in charge of him till Mum and Dad came home, but Mum had asked him to sort out his old toys and games and given him a list of things to get from the shop. He spent an hour or two rummaging through the things he'd stuffed into a cupboard until it was time to go out.

His crossing of the green was carefully timed to coincide with playtime at school. Just as he'd hoped, Simon and some other Year Six boys were in the playground, leaning against the wall, as it was still too hot for football.

'Hey, Simon!' Henry yelled, and Simon came over, followed by Neil, Jonathan and Elissa.

'Aren't you bored, hanging round at home?' Neil asked.

Henry shrugged, not liking to be the centre of attention. 'S'all right. But I'd rather be here with you lot.'

'Can't you come in with us after play?' Elissa suggested. She had her long hair in two plaits today. Jonathan waggled the end of one and said, 'Don't be daft, Liss.'

'You could, though, on Wednesday!' Simon gave his big Rusty Dobbs grin. 'Miss Murphy always goes on a course, Wednesdays.'

'Mrs Mobbs takes us, she's a supply teacher. She can never remember all our names,' Elissa joined in.

'And Tim's away this week, so there's an empty place next to me,' Simon finished.

Henry thought about it, liking the idea. 'But how can I? I won't have any books or anything, will I?'

'No prob,' Simon said, with the air of someone who had everything sorted. 'We don't work in books any more. We're doing stuff on paper, for a special folder that goes to our new school.'

'And we're not really doing proper work now, anyway,' Elissa added. 'Only quizzes and team games and things, cos it's nearly end of term.'

'Well, I think you're all off your trolley.'

Jonathan put a finger to the side of his head in a *screwy* gesture. 'Trying to smuggle someone into school! If I had an extra week's holiday, I wouldn't be moaning about it.'

'I wasn't,' Henry began, but all the others were so pleased with the plan that they began saying, 'Henry the Stowaway!' and looking round for other people to let in on the secret.

'And, Henry,' Elissa pleaded, her small face earnest, 'will you be in our relay team on Saturday? Simon, Neil and me?'

'What's Saturday?'

'It's the village fête and sports,' Simon told him. 'Everyone'll be there. There's all sorts of stalls and games and competitions – it's great!'

By the time the bell went for the end of break, Henry had agreed not only to smuggle himself into school but also to join the relay team on Saturday and have a go at Wellie Whanging. He felt much more cheerful as he walked home.

Later, when he'd finished sorting and went round to Pat's, Dottie was out in the garden. Although she looked pale and tired, she was sitting in her chair as usual, knitting. Her twiggy fingers moved without stopping, pushing the wool forward, dipping a needle to catch the new stitch, passing it on. On the garden table, the Scrabble board was set out, in the middle of a game. Pat had gone in to answer a phone call.

'Well, Henry love, and how you keeping?' Dottie asked.

'OK, thanks.' He knew he ought to ask how she was, but couldn't. Her illness and oldness frightened him, as if she hovered on the edge of something he couldn't understand. 'It's the village fête on Saturday,' he told her, for something to say. There were questions he wanted to ask, but he couldn't come straight out with them. 'Will you go?'

'Ooh yes! Wouldn't miss it for anything.' Dottie yanked at her wool, which had got hooked round the chair leg. 'I do like a nice fête!'

'I'm going to run in the relay,' Henry told her.

'Good! I'll be there to cheer you on,' Dottie said. 'Long as you don't expect me to run in the grown-ups' race!'

Henry laughed. She gave him one of her straight looks and said, 'You won't believe it, but I used to be a fast runner, in my day. I could run faster than any of the boys in my class.'

'Like Grace,' Henry said. Simon had told him that she'd been the fastest runner in the school when she was in Year 6.

'Well, I was quite like Grace when I was her age,' Dottie agreed. 'She reminds me of me.'

Henry was shocked into silence. How could that be true? Grace was horrible, and Dottie was Dottie – he couldn't see any likeness.

'You've got to admire her spirit, haven't you?' Dottie went on. 'If she wants to do something, you can bet she'll do it.'

Henry sat down on the grass and picked at a daisy stem. An unpleasant feeling fizzed in his chest. *You've got to admire her spirit.* Grace's spirit? All Henry could think of was Grace's mouth and the mean things that came out of it. It wasn't fair that Dottie should say such nice things about her! He'd never heard Grace say a kind word about Dottie. Not once.

Dottie looked at him, and said softly, 'You want to stand up to her a bit more. Give her as good as she hands out.'

'She calls me names,' Henry grumped. 'Strawberry Pip and Squidge.'

'I used to be called Pipsqueak at school,' Dottie said, 'because I was so small. That's not to say people didn't like me. I think most of them *did* like me. What d'you reckon?'

Henry didn't answer. He couldn't imagine anyone not liking Dottie; but she'd got it completely wrong if she was trying to say that Grace liked *him*. She'd called him a little kid, hadn't she?

Hadn't wanted him to tag along at the air display. How could she make it any more obvious?

'Grace is all right,' Dottie said; 'just going through a spiky stage. Now look at this.' She waved her knitting towards the Scrabble board. 'I'm on a winning streak here. All my letters out in one go – that's fifty extra points!'

Henry looked at the tiles that spelled out THIR-TEEN along the bottom of the board.

'I had "THIRTEE" sitting on my rack and then Pat went and put down that "N" in just the right place where I could use it. And it's a triple word score,' Dottie said proudly. 'Thirty-six for the word and then the extra fifty – that's eighty-six. Best score I've ever got!'

'That's brilliant!' Henry said, kneeling up to look at the score-sheet.

'Don't you go jogging the board now, spoiling it,' Dottie warned. 'I've never managed that before.'

Henry sat down again. He wanted to ask Dottie whether she'd heard the aircraft noise in the night. Stupid question, because how could she have heard twelve flying Lancasters? Instead, he said, 'You know the other day? You started telling us about meeting someone called Henry when you came to live here?'

Dottie's fingers carried on knitting and she

looked at the Scrabble board without showing any sign of having heard. Then she said, 'Didn't I finish telling you? Thought I had. Yes, Henry the Navigator. That's what I called him.'

'Why?' Henry remembered maps of the world he'd seen on the wall of his old classroom, with arrows across the seas showing voyage routes. 'Was he an explorer?'

'No, love,' Dottie said. 'Not like you mean, anyway, though I suppose he was in a way. He was in the RAF. He flew in them Lancasters.'

'Oh, like Simon's Grandad – Great-grandad! Was he at Lakenfield?'

'No,' Dottie said. 'He was based at this other airfield near here. Risingheath, it was called. It's all derelict now.'

Coldness fluttered down Henry's spine. 'Was he a pilot?'

'No, love.' Dottie shook out her skein so that a length of green wool unravelled itself. 'He was a navigator. Henry the Navigator. He was the one that worked out the maps and the wind and the speed and suchlike and told the pilot where to fly.'

Of course. Simon had told him about the different jobs people did, seven crew to every Lancaster. Henry was Henry the Navigator. Henry's brain was working rapidly – like puzzling away at something in maths when the beginning of the answer dangled itself in his mind and he had to cling tightly to the thread of thought, because if he let go, it would slip away and be gone.

'Did everyone here have something to do with the war?' he asked.

Dottie nodded. 'Felt like that, sometimes! The pub was full of RAF folk every night – there was people billeted in the village. It went on for nearly six years, you know, got to be a way of life. Even farming was war work, then. Told you I worked in an aircraft factory, didn't I? Girls and women did all sorts of jobs, it wasn't just the men. Girls did driving, engineering, aircraft maintenance, things we hadn't dreamed of doing before. Course there was the army and the navy as well, but up here in Suffolk it was all flying. Handy for the coast, you see. It's just across the North Sea to Germany.'

'To drop bombs?'

'That's right. Awful, it was. People over there getting bombed, same as we was in the Blitz, and our young lads being sent off to drop bombs over their side. You're lucky,' Dottie said. 'You won't have to live through anything like that, fingers crossed.'

'He must have been brave,' Henry said, in a small voice.

'Brave?' Dottie tilted her head on one side, considering. 'Yes, he was. And you know what was so brave? It was because he was scared to death every time he climbed into that plane. He never told me, but I knew.'

'But how could he be both?' Henry couldn't help asking. 'Brave *and* scared?'

'Well, who in their right mind wouldn't be scared? Knowing the odds?' Dottie said, a touch sharply. 'You wouldn't *need* to be brave if you didn't see the dangers, would you?' Then she gave him a sideways look and said, 'Odd thing is, you remind me of him. Reminded me soon as I saw you. And not just being called Henry. Same dark hair, same brown eyes. Same cheeky smile.'

Henry couldn't get his head round that. Henry the Navigator was a grown-up man, an RAF man in uniform, a man who could find the way to Germany and back in the dark in a Lancaster bomber. How could Dottie see Henry in him?

'Was he the one you were going to marry?' he asked. He glanced at the kitchen door, hoping Pat wouldn't come out. Not till Dottie had finished telling him.

'Yes, love, he was.' Dottie stopped knitting for a moment and looked over the garden fence towards the orchard. 'Met him over at Risingheath. I used to help out in the NAAFI van at the airfield.'

'Naffy van?' Henry repeated.

'Yes, that's right – sort of mobile canteen. It stood for . . . now, what was it? . . . Navy, Army, Airforce, Something-or-other . . . First clapped eyes on Henry when I served him a mug of tea and a doughnut.'

'It cost tuppence,' Henry said. The words were out of his mouth before he knew he was going to say them.

'Well, and how would you know that?' Dottie said, staring.

'I – I just guessed.' He could have said: and Henry dropped his change in the grass and had to grovel about to find it. I was there!

'Two old pence, it would have been,' Dottie said. 'That's – what? A bit less than a penny now. Anyway, that's how we met. He kept coming to the NAAFI van. I liked him but I was too shy to tell him. Then we met again at a dance. He came over and asked me to dance and from then on I never wanted to dance with anyone else. He was only a boy really, not much older than me. And then, when we got to know each other, he used to come over to the village to meet me, when he had nights off flying. It was a long, hot summer, just like this one. We'd go walking together in the woods and down by the stream. Courting, we called it then. Sounds so old fashioned, doesn't it?'

Henry unravelled a creeping buttercup that had flattened itself among the grasses. A dizzy feeling came over him as he thought of his dream. 'What happened to him? Why didn't you get married after all?'

'He never came back,' Dottie said. 'He'd flown twelve times, him and his crew. Twelve times over the North Sea or right over Germany, with the anti-aircraft guns and the fighters. Each time, he was so relieved to get back safely, but he knew he'd got to do it all over again and again and again. Once you'd done thirty, you'd be stood down for a rest. Well, they'd done twelve and they was getting themselves a bit worked up about Unlucky Thirteen. Nineteen forty-three, this was. Come to think of it, it was just this time – middle of July. Well, Henry always said he wasn't superstitious, but you couldn't blame him, could you? Knowing what the odds were. "If I get back from this one," he said, "we'll go into Ipswich and get you an engagement ring". And I said, "*When*, you mean, not *if*." And he just shook his head. He'd been trying to look cheerful, but all of a sudden this look came over his face and I could tell.'

'Tell what?'

Dottie looked across at the orchard again. 'All of a sudden he knew. He knew he wasn't coming back.'

'What happened to him?' Henry asked.

'I never found out,' Dottie said bleakly. 'No one ever knew. They just flew off that night, the seven of them in that Lanc, and never came back. I watched them go from my bedroom window in the Rectory. Lancs taking off, climbing, one after the other. And I listened for them coming back over, in the early hours. I'd counted them out and I counted them back in. Three planes went missing that night and one of them was Henry and his crew. No one knew what happened. No one saw anything. No radio message.'

'Nothing?' Henry thought of all the Lancaster bombers he'd seen – or dreamed about, last night, flying into the clouds and fading, as if dissolving into mist. But real planes didn't dissolve. 'Still? After all those years?'

'Nothing.' Dottie shook her head sadly. 'There were so many ways it could have happened. They could have been shot to pieces or crashed into the sea or burst into flames. When aircrew went missing like that, you didn't necessarily know they'd been killed – they could have landed in the sea and managed to get into their lifeboat or they could have bailed out and been taken prisoner in Germany. So you didn't stop hoping, not till after the war ended and all the prisoners came home – you hoped there'd be a letter or a telegram or they'd just turn up. But I never did find out. They must have been killed, all of them, and I'll never know how.'

Henry's stomach churned at the thought of all the things that could happen to a Lancaster bomber in wartime. He looked at the word THIR-TEEN on the Scrabble board and saw Dottie looking at it too. She nodded slowly.

'Last time I saw him, he said, "See you here, same time tomorrow. I'll be waiting," he said, "whatever happens". And I thought at the time, well, that's an odd thing to say – because of, you know, all the things that *could* happen. But he promised he'd be waiting and he wasn't. He never came back.'

'Couldn't you have married someone else, after the war?' Henry asked, although he was glad she hadn't.

Dottie shook her head. 'I had my chances. But nothing else seemed quite the same, somehow, as me and Henry. Anyway, I'd promised and it wasn't a promise I ever wanted to break. My Henry, he made things come alive for me in a way no one else could. He made me see things. We'd be walking along in the woods and suddenly he'd stop and listen, and say: "There's a tree-creeper. Listen!" And then we'd look round and see it. And a couple of nights, walking back to the village, we saw a barn owl. Floating up to the trees like a great flake of snow. Once or twice there was nightingales. I didn't know none of that, coming from the East End of London – couldn't have told you a nightingale from a house sparrow. It was Henry showed me.' She sighed. 'Nineteen forty-three, this was. This week, in nineteen forty-three. Such a long time ago. And I sometimes wonder what my Henry would think if he saw me now. There's him, a good-looking young chap of twenty-two, and me a doddery old lady! But you know, sometimes I still get the sense he's there waiting for me, where he always waited. Where he said he'd wait. Daft, isn't it?'

'Where? Where would he wait?' Henry asked, though he already knew the answer. He knew that the man he'd seen was Henry the Navigator, just as he knew that the bombers he'd heard last night were the bombers in Dottie's memory.

'By the gate out there in the orchard,' Dottie said. 'The firefly gate, we called it. Though they was really glow-worms, like I said. That's where we used to wait for each other. Meet you at the firefly gate, we'd say. Mrs Simmonds, who lived in your house back then, used to call it Henry's Haunt, he was there so often.'

If he wanted to, Henry could say: 'He does wait.

He does haunt. I've seen him, waiting there. Waiting for you. Perhaps he's waiting there now. And I've dreamed it all, the canteen and the tea and the doughnut and the tuppence. I saw bombers, I heard them. Last night. Twelve Lancaster bombers flying over and nine coming back.' Something weird was happening. Dottie's thoughts and memories and the other Henry's were getting themselves all mixed up with his. And a sense of black dread coursed through him, blotting out the sun and the grass and the garden. *Your turn next. My turn.* Something terrible was going to happen and he had no way of stopping it. He lay back and looked up at the sky, but it was so huge that he felt he would fall into it and be lost for ever; his stomach reeled, as if he were tumbling through miles and miles of empty air. He rolled over on his front and closed his eyes to stop himself throwing up. There was a cold tremble all the way down his arms and his legs. He tried to swallow, tried to breathe normally.

'Hey! You OK, lovey - a touch too much sun?'

Dottie's voice seemed to reach him from a long way away. But now Pat was coming across the grass, saying, 'OK then, Dottie. Let's finish this game. You'd better help me, Henry. She's beating me by miles.'

Henry blinked and sat up. By looking at the Scrabble board and the tea-tray, he could push back the feeling of dread; but whatever it was, it was still there waiting for him. *Your turn next. My turn.*

While he was gazing at Pat's rack of letters, something occurred to him. He must get Simon's great-grandfather – Rusty Dobbs or Lucky Dobbs or whatever his real name was – to come over and talk to Dottie. Because if it was the same Rusty Dobbs in the dream, and if Henry had been Henry, then they knew each other. And maybe it had been on Henry the Navigator's thirteenth flight that Rusty Dobbs had got flu. Good luck for Lucky Dobbs, bad luck for Henry.

Pat's letters were EDITHCD. There was a word there if only he could find it.

TWELVE

Two-face Grace

'If you're writing back,' Dad said, when Henry showed him Nabil's postcard and cartoon, 'you can ask if he'd like to come and stay.'

'Can I? Great!'

'When would be a good time?' Dad asked Mum.

They were in the middle of eating. Mum got up to glance at the calendar on its hook above the fridge. 'Last week in August?'

Dad nodded. 'Fine with me.'

'By the way,' Mum said, sitting down again, 'I'm staying at home tomorrow – the plumber's coming. I thought it'd be nice to invite Grace for tea.'

Henry pulled a face. 'Yeukk! Do we have to?'

'Henry!' Dad reproved.

They were having salad and new potatoes with butter. Henry loved these usually, but now he started rolling the small potatoes around with his fork instead of eating them. A happy thought occurred to him. 'She won't want to come, anyway.'

'I'm sure she will,' Mum said. 'With Dottie ill, it can't be very cheerful in her house. She'll probably be glad of the change.'

Huh! Henry thought. Grace was the one who was always sulking. It'd be far more fun to have Dottie round for tea.

'What's the problem, Henry?' Dad said. 'Don't you like Grace?'

'She's such a nice girl,' Mum said.

Henry prodded a tomato with his fork. *'Nice!'*

'Bit bossy, is she?' Dad said knowingly. 'You want to stand up to her, Hen. Don't let her walk all over you.'

'Don't call me Hen,' Henry muttered. He could imagine it all too clearly: Grace and her friend Tracy calling him Mother Hen or Kentucky Fried, flapping their wings and making chook-chook noises whenever they got on the coach. The Strawberry variations were bad enough.

'You ought to make more effort to be nice to her,' Dad said. 'Perhaps she's shy. She always strikes me as a bit awkward. Not necessarily unfriendly.'

Shy! Grace? Henry nearly snorted into his lettuce.

'Besides,' Mum said, 'you want Nabil to stay, Dad and I want Grace to come to tea. That's fair, isn't it?'

Henry clung to the hope that Grace wouldn't want to come or would be busy doing something else tomorrow. As soon as the plates were cleared, Mum made him go round to Pat's to ask. Grace, not surprisingly, wasn't overwhelmed with excitement at the idea; she just said, 'Oh, all right. Might as well.'

'How kind of your mum and dad! Grace'll enjoy it, won't you, dear?' Pat said.

Another one who'd got it all wrong.

Winding Henry up was Grace's speciality. When she came round next day, she was so nice and polite that he wanted to hit her. Mum would never believe how nasty she could be.

Grace had clearly decided to be on best behaviour. She admired the work Mum and Dad had done in the garden, said how scrummy Mum's blackcurrant cheesecake was and had a second slice. She only called him Strawberry once, by mistake, but she managed to make it sound like a friendly nickname, and Mum *laughed*. It just wasn't fair!

Henry hadn't told Mum how she'd tried to make him fall off Amber and break his neck. They wouldn't believe him if he told them. They'd say, 'No, no, Grace is such a nice little girl. You must have got it all wrong.'

Even when Mum asked, 'How's your Aunt Dottie, Grace? Any better?' she didn't shrug in her usual sulky way, as if she couldn't care less. She said, 'Well, she's not too bad today, but she's got to go into hospital next week. It's something to do with her heart. She has to keep going for tests.'

And she sat there all serious-faced while Mum made sympathetic noises. Henry didn't understand. If Dottie was only going into hospital to have tests, that must mean it wasn't all that serious, mustn't it? Having tests didn't mean you were going to *die*.

'Why don't you show Grace the quiz game on the computer, Henry?' Mum said after tea.

'Oh, yes please, Str-Henry,' Grace said, polite as anything.

Mum stayed in the kitchen, clearing up, while Henry and Grace settled down by the computer in the front room. Henry expected that as soon as Mum was out of earshot, Grace would go back to being her normal self, but instead she got really involved in the quiz, grabbing the mouse when it was her turn and shouting out the answers.

'That was great!' she said when they'd finished.

114

'Oh, yeah,' Henry jeered. 'You would say that, cos you won. It's not such a brilliant score, twenty-five. I got more than that last time.'

'Want another game, then?'

'No, I don't.' Henry grabbed the mouse and clicked EXIT. 'You're so – so – two-faced!' he burst out. 'All this *yes, thank you* and *no, thank you* and *lovely, thank you* like you're an angel or something. Two-Face Grace, that's what you are! And pretending to care about Dottie! It's never bothered you before. I've never even seen you speak to her—'

'What do you know?' Grace burst out. She turned to look at him and to his astonishment her eyes filled with tears. Big, shiny tears that swelled and brimmed on the edge of her lower lashes till one spilled over and splashed on to her cheek. She brushed at it angrily and turned her face away. Just then, Dad came in at the front door, hot from the car, with his tie pulled loose and shirt-sleeves rolled up.

'Hi, you two!' he said brightly. 'Having a good game?'

'Yes, thank you,' Grace said, wiping her nose on her sleeve. 'It's a really good quiz. I was just going to tell Henry, we've got Flight Simulation at home. Dad's borrowed it from someone. It's a bit old fashioned, but it's still OK. You can have a go on it when you come round tomorrow, Henry.'

Henry couldn't make her out at all. And as if he hadn't had enough to put up with, he got told off when Grace had gone home for not making her welcome. Mum and Dad both ganged up on him.

'She was making a real effort to be nice to you! And all you did was look grumpy and sulk,' Mum told him. 'If you won't be friendly back, what do you expect?'

'She looked quite upset when I came in. Almost in tears,' Dad said. 'What were you saying to her?'

'Nothing!' Henry said hotly.

'She's anxious about Dottie being so ill, I think,' Mum said quietly. 'You must try to be a bit more considerate, Hen.'

'Tell you what,' Henry grouched, 'why don't you get Grace to move in, and I'll move out?' He heard the way his voice sounded – rude and sulky, just as they'd said.

THIRTEEN

Intruanter

By Wednesday, Simon had spread the word to everyone in 6M that Henry would be a class stow-away, so that no one would draw attention to him. Meeting him at the gates, Simon handed him a spare green sweatshirt. 'There you are – school uni-form. Not that you'll need it today, it's going to be boiling. What about Grace's Mum? What've you told her?'

'Sorted,' Henry said, though he had an uneasy feeling he was going to be caught out. 'I just said there was a change of plan and I'm in school today.'

There were whispers, giggles and nudges as Henry sat down in the spare seat next to Simon. When Mrs Mobbs, the supply teacher, called the register, no one pointed out that there was one extra person in the class. From the name, Henry had pictured Mrs Mobbs as grey and grandmotherly, but she was nothing like that. Yes, she had grey hair, but it was cut very short and boyishly and she wore track pants and trainers like a PE teacher.

'Just watch out at playtime and lunch,' Simon warned him. 'Don't draw attention to yourself—'

'As if I would!'

'No, but you know what I mean. Whichever teacher's on playground duty might wonder who you are, even if Mrs Mobbs won't.'

The morning was fun. It was after lunch that things went wrong.

Afternoon assembly with the head teacher, Mrs Tregarth, was the most likely time for Henry to be noticed, but Year Six were right at the back of the hall, and no one paid them much attention. Mrs Tregarth wore a long dress with huge red poppies on it, which made her look rather holidayish, but she had the sort of soft voice that sounded as if it could turn firm when necessary. Next they had rounders, out on the big field, and although Jenny forgot herself enough to shout, 'Go, Henry!' when he managed to give the ball a flukey hard whack that sent it soaring and gave him time for a whole rounder, Mrs Mobbs didn't seem to notice. Then there was play, and after-wards art.

Mrs Mobbs's art lesson sent everyone back out to the field, to look at the long grasses that grew at the edges and bring back at least six different kinds to draw or paint. 'There's only one kind of grass, isn't there?' Simon whispered to Henry. 'Green stuff.' But no, there wasn't. Mrs Mobbs had already started her own collection and had put it in a vase like a proper flower arrangement. She placed the vase carefully underneath one of the lights so that everyone could see how beautiful the flowering grasses were.

'So you think it's just green stuff, do you, Stephen?' Her grasp of names might be poor, but her hearing was sharp as a cat's. 'Green stuff to play football on? Well, it's not. Not this time of year, when it flowers. Come and look at all the colours here.'

Peering closely, Henry had to admit that he'd never properly looked at grass before. There were purples and silvers and browns, shimmering in the light; there were silky strands and silvery tufts and golden beards and plump seeds like oats. He wanted to run his fingers through the grass water-fall.

'Off you go. See what you can find.' Mrs Mobbs

119

waved them out of the door. 'Ten minutes, then back here. I got all these from just one roadside verge.'

By now – the last session of the school day – Henry had almost forgotten that he had no right to be at school. He, Simon and Jonathan wandered round the field's edges, collecting their grasses, then returned past the big hall windows towards the classroom.

'Hey, we haven't got this one,' Simon was saying, darting towards a fringe of long grass that had been left uncut beside the building.

'Simon Dobbs!'

The voice made him jump back abruptly to where Jonathan and Henry were standing with their grasses. Henry almost dropped his bundle; but there was nowhere to hide. Mrs Tregarth, the head teacher, appeared at the open window. *You dingbat, Simon!* he thought, not knowing whether to shrivel up or to run away fast. He'd led him right past the head's window!

'Who's that boy with you?' Mrs Tregarth sounded puzzled rather than angry.

Simon blushed scarlet. 'It's Henry, Miss,' he mumbled.

'Henry?'

'He'll be in our year at Hartsfield. He came with

us on Tuesday, so I thought it'd be OK for him to come to school for the day,' Simon explained.

Mrs Tregarth looked astonished. 'Oh, you did, did you? I think you'd better come in here, all three of you. Jonathan, go back to your classroom first and tell Mrs Mobbs you're with me.'

'Duhh!' Henry couldn't help saying it, as he and Simon entered the building through the glass doors of the hall.

'You don't have to tell me.' Even the tips of Simon's ears were bright red. Henry felt himself panicking as they approached the office door. He hated being told off – even by someone who wasn't actually *his* head teacher. What on earth was he going to say?

'Come on in and sit down.' Mrs Tregarth left the door ajar for Jonathan, and pulled over an extra chair. 'So you're Henry, are you? Henry Stirling, isn't it?'

'Yes,' said Henry, staring at the red poppies on her dress.

'Come in, Jonathan. Sit down. Now where—'

'It's not his fault, Miss, honest—' Simon tried to interrupt, but Mrs Tregarth shushed him and said, 'Henry can speak for himself, I'm sure.'

Henry began to feel a little better. Mrs Tregarth didn't look as if she was going to be angry; she nodded and even smiled while he explained that he'd just wanted to join the others for the day. Then she turned to Simon and Jonathan.

'So! You two can claim responsibility for this bright idea, can you?'

Jonathan looked sidelong at Simon, who said, 'It was me.'

'Well, Simon, it's very kind of you to take it on yourself to make arrangements for Henry, and I'm sure Henry's pleased to have made friends so quickly. But you have to understand that we can't have people coming into school quite unaccounted for. The teachers and I are responsible for everyone in school – that's why we take registers morning and afternoon. That's why we have fire drills. That's why all visitors have to sign in and out and wear a badge while they're on the premises. We can't be responsible for someone we don't even know is here. You understand that, don't you?'

Mumbled yeses.

'And what's more, I think you've taken unfair advantage of Mrs Mobbs. Simon, you know you'd never have got away with this if Miss Murphy had been taking the class as usual. It was a bit sneaky, don't you think?'

A barely audible yes from Simon.

'Henry, I'm going to have to phone your parents

to explain what's happened today. But what I'm going to suggest is that I phone the authority and ask for special permission for you to attend school for the last two days of term – since you're so keen to be here.' She looked at him kindly. 'It's a big change, isn't it, leaving primary school? You might as well enjoy the last two days. Simon and Jonathan, go back to your classroom. As soon as the bell goes I want you back in here. I'll tell Mrs Mobbs what's happened and you can apologise for messing her about. Henry, you stay here while I make some phone calls.'

Simon gave a rueful backward glance as he slipped out of the door behind Jonathan, abandoning Henry. But Mrs Tregarth smiled at him and said, 'Well! I've heard of people truanting *out* of school, but this is the first time I've had someone truanting *in!*'

FOURTEEN

Henry the Navigator

Henry had another telling-off from Mum and Dad –
but not too serious, as he could tell they thought
it quite funny that he'd smuggled himself into
school. Mrs Tregarth had phoned the education
authority, and for the last two days of term Henry
was added to the class list as a visitor. To Class
6M, though, he was Henry the Stowaway, Henry
the Illegal Immigrant. Oddly, it made him quite
popular.

'Here's the boy who loves school so much he
couldn't bear to stay away!' Miss Murphy greeted
him. 'Simon, are you sure there's no one else you'd
like to invite to join the fun?'

The lessons today were hardly lessons – there was
a team quiz, with prizes, and then a coach trip to
the swimming-pool (Mrs Tregarth had told Henry

to bring swimming things) and, lastly, making a huge collage on a whole side of the hall. Henry was looking forward to tomorrow, when everyone was bringing food for a party, and there was going to be a special visit from a theatre company.

The weather, though, didn't match his cheerful mood at all. The sky turned so dark and heavy that Miss Murphy had to put the hall lights on. By home-time, as Henry waved goodbye to Simon and Elissa and walked across to Pat's, the bruised, purplish-grey clouds seemed to be smothering the village, and the first rain-drops – fat and warm – were spitting at the dry, dusty ground. Henry had the uneasy sense of something bad waiting to happen. A low, thundery growl rumbled in the distance.

Grace, holding her school bag over her head, ran up the path behind him while he waited for Pat to answer the door. She pushed past Henry and dumped her bag, with only a grudging 'Hi' to her mother. Henry hadn't seen her yesterday, as she'd gone to Tracy's after school. Since Tuesday he'd been looking forward to trying out the flight simulation game; he hoped she hadn't forgotten.

Pat put a finger to her lips in a shushing gesture – not that anyone was making any noise – and told them that Dottie was lying down in her room. 'She's not feeling too good. Must be this muggy weather. If it's going to rain, that'll clear the air, I hope. Might make her feel better.'

'Aunt Dottie's always ill,' Grace grumbled.

Henry gave her a hard look, which she didn't even notice. So much for being upset about Dottie, he thought. She was Two-Face Grace, all right.

'I suppose you're going to say don't use the computer?' Grace whinged, pausing on the bottom stair.

'No, you can, as long as you keep the sound right down,' Pat said.

Grace ran on up; Henry dithered, not sure what to do, with Dottie in bed and no one in the garden.

'Why don't you go up too, Henry?' Pat suggested. 'Grace can show you the game John's borrowed for her.'

'All right.' Henry knew Grace didn't want him, but he'd put up with that to get a look at the flight programme.

The door to the back room – Dottie's room – was closed. Grace was clumping about in the room above. In Henry's house this was the attic, reached only by a trap-door, but here it had been converted into an extra bedroom with its own narrow flight of stairs. Reaching the top landing, Henry saw that the extra storey was all one room, with walls that sloped with the angle of the roof. Slanting windows, on the garden side, let in light. The room contained Grace's bed, some bookshelves, a curtained-off hanging space and the desk with the computer on it. There was a Tornado poster on one of the sloping walls. Grace was sitting on the only chair.

'What're you doing up here?' She gave him a disparaging glance before turning back to the screen.

'Come to see the flight simulation. You said—'

'Yeah, right. You can get better ones than this now, but it's still good practice for me. Like being a real trainee pilot. You can watch if you like.'

On to the screen came a row of dials, below a view of a runway seen head on. It was all amazingly detailed and realistic. From the computer's speakers came the sound of an idling engine, reminding Henry of his Lancaster dream. The sound merged with the thunder that was grumbling in the distance like a lion about to stir itself. Butterflies quivered in Henry's stomach as if he really were going to fly. He had only flown twice in his life, to Ireland and back, and he remembered how anxious he'd been. It would be different if he under*stood*. How could such an enormous metal machine, full of people and luggage, get into the air and stay there?

'I'm going to take off,' Grace said. 'You use the mouse, like this, see.' She demonstrated various movements. 'Watch this.'

RELEASE PARKING BRAKES appeared on the screen above the dials. Grace clicked the mouse and Henry watched as the dotted line along the centre of the runway began to move towards him, faster and faster, as the engine noise increased. He heard the plane lift off. Now he was looking down at the criss-cross runways of the airfield, which tilted and fell out of view as the plane banked. He was flying out, over the sea. He could see the coastline dipping and rising as Grace made the plane swerve, using the mouse and keys.

'Can I have a go?' he asked, torn between nervousness and an itch to sit in the pilot's seat.

'Wait till I've finished,' Grace said impatiently.

Then, above the engine noise, they heard Pat's voice from the landing below, whisper-shouting because of Dottie. 'Grace! Gracie? Come down here a minute!'

Grace tutted, then passed the mouse over to Henry. 'OK, you can take over. But only till I come back.'

She went down the twisty stairs, out of sight.

Henry could only think about the buzzing sensation in his ears and the fluttering in his stomach. He hoped he wasn't going to heave. With an effort, he made himself swallow, and the buzzing cleared a little. It was always like this – fighting himself, trying to get the better of his own fear. The plane was flying level now, into the darkness, but he knew from his instrument panel that the water was eight thousand feet below, and the English coast two miles ahead. To the others, he was Henry the Navigator, always calm, always working away at his calculations and his compass bearings; but perhaps they all shared the same sick terror that was only just kept under control.

That stupid song came into his mind, the one they sang in the mess: *They scraped him off the runway like a dollop of strawberry jam* . . . He hated that song; it made him feel sick to think about it, but when the others sang it he joined in anyway and pretended to laugh – as if he didn't care, as if crashes were something to joke about.

All day, he'd had a bad feeling about tonight, with Rusty out of action, in sick bay with flu. The crew had always flown together, the seven of them, mates, for each of their twelve flights. This was number thirteen and, instead of Rusty, they had Ian Davy, a new flight engineer straight from training. At least they still had Skipper, a safe pair of hands if ever there was one.

You should never let yourself think you'd made it, not till you were safely on the runway, not even then . . .

When the impact came – jarring all sense out of him – his first coherent thought in the confusion was that he'd been expecting it. A fighter? Another bomber? There was no way of knowing. All he knew was that the aircraft had dropped abruptly and was yawing to the left, that he'd been thrown right out of his seat and there was a cold wind tearing through the fuselage. *This is it, this is it,* he thought, covering his ears, waiting for the implosion into the sea that would surely be the last thing he ever knew. Then, slowly, he registered that the plane was still flying, though God alone knew on what course. Somehow he was unhurt, but while he staggered to his feet he was being grabbed and pulled forward.

'You'll have to take over!' It was Jackson, the wireless operator: shouting, frantic. 'You'll have to take over! Skipper's right out of it and the new lad's hurt bad. The back's shot to pieces. It's you or no one.'

Henry had done some flying during his training, but had never flown a Lanc before, let alone a seriously damaged one in darkness over the North Sea. Oddly, though, he felt less afraid now – with the plane almost falling to bits around him – than he had earlier, wrapped up in superstitious fears. The Lanc was still flying, somehow, and if anyone was going to get it down – and save the others on board, however many of them were still alive – it would have to be him.

Jackson dragged the unconscious Skipper out of his seat and Henry groped himself into position. He gripped the control wheel and stared at the row of dials, at the flickering needles. All sense had been knocked out of them too: airspeed zero? That was nonsense for a start. But the Flight Engineer – the new young chap, Rusty's stand-in – was slumped lifeless against the wing-spar. It was bitterly cold in the cockpit. Henry felt blasted by icy air; the heating system had packed up altogether.

'If you can just nurse the old kite back to the coast,' Jackson said, 'we might make it.'

'You'd better bale out,' Henry told him. 'You and anyone else who can.' It was a horrible prospect – the jump into the dark, the cold sea – but the chance of survival would be greater than staying in a plane that might burn up, disintegrate or crash-land.

Jackson, peering at the dials beside him, shook his head. 'We're staying put. All of us.'

Henry adjusted his feet on the rudder pedals and opened the throttles a little. The plane creaked and groaned in protest. Squinting, he could see nothing below, nothing at all. It was like flying into a black well, even if logic told him that every second was a second nearer home and safety. They might stay up here for ever, hanging on, coaxing the wounded aircraft – but then he looked at the fuel gauge and realised that of course they couldn't. They'd have to come down, somewhere. And if they didn't strike the coast soon, it would be in the sea.

They scraped him off the runway . . . Well, that was one thing he needn't worry about. There wasn't going to be any runway, just the sea. The North Sea, all of it . . .

'Getting a bit lighter now,' Jackson said.

Straining his eyes, Henry saw a line of foam and dark shore beyond.

'We can make it. We can.' Jackson was only whispering, not daring to say it out loud. But all Henry could think was: *Unlucky thirteen. Unlucky thirteen. We're not down yet.*

He was aiming for the black rim of coast. As soon

132

as they'd crossed it, he'd look for a level field, somewhere he could bring the plane down. It would be a messy landing but with luck they wouldn't actually crash. They'd have to hitch a lift back to Risingheath when it was properly daylight. He'd promised Dottie . . .

If only he could see somewhere clear of trees . . .

He was letting the aircraft lose height, its failing engines giving up the struggle. His ears went fuzzy as the plane dropped steadily; all the time his eyes were searching the gloom. He saw the whiteness of surf as they crossed the coast at a sharp angle. The darkness was retreating slowly, washed with palest pink as dawn approached. Henry was staring, staring, till he thought his eyeballs would burst with the strain.

Then he saw it: straight ahead, directly in the flight path. A small town, clustered round a church tower. Roads spreading out like a map. Not a light showing, the blackout in perfect order. Henry thought of people asleep in bed, unaware of the Lancaster bomber that was about to crash-land in their midst.

Unless he did something.

Jackson saw it at the same time. 'Get the nose up!'

'I'm trying—'

He hauled at the throttles with all his strength, hoping to infuse life into the dying plane. Jackson staggered and fell back against the navigation desk. Henry saw the horizon tilt at a crazy angle. His weight thrown to one side, he had to struggle to keep his seat, bracing himself into it. Someone was shouting at him, but the plane was going into a banking dive he could do nothing to control. They were veering over the scrubland and the beaches, nose down, aiming straight at the sea. Henry heaved at the throttles, knowing the plane couldn't respond. Hopeless even to think of making a landing now; too late to bale out.

His hands moved uselessly at the controls. The sea tilted up to slam itself at the plane. He knew he couldn't survive the crash; none of them would.

This is it, then . . . my turn . . .

Unlucky thirteen . . .

He thought of Rusty Dobbs, safe in bed in sick bay. The seconds stretched out while he waited. He thought of Dottie, her hair streaming as she ran to meet him, her special smile that was just for him . . .

Then all his senses exploded in a starburst of dark.

The image on the screen splintered into fragments.

Henry heard the impact, heard the fuselage splitting and smashing, saw bits of broken plane bob up on the computer screen. For a moment there was silence, then the picture reformed itself into the starting position, the row of dials, the runway stretching ahead, and the command RELEASE PARKING BRAKES. The sound was of an idling engine, ready to start all over again. Henry looked down at his hands on the keyboard, then round at Grace's bed and the poster on the wall. It was raining hard outside, battering the sloping window.

'Strawberry! Pip!' Grace's feet were thudding up the stairs. 'Didn't you hear me yelling? I've called you at least six times. Mum says we've got to unplug the computer and come down cos the thunderstorm's coming nearer.'

Henry glanced dizzily at the window and saw it lit up by a double flash of sheet lightning. Impatient, Grace leaned over to grab the mouse and clicked it several times. The flight simulation screen disappeared and she switched off the computer, then unplugged it from the wall socket. 'Come on. What's the matter? You're not frightened of a bit of lightning, are you?'

'No.' Henry got slowly to his feet. He followed Grace down, wondering whether anyone would believe him – whether he believed it himself – if he said that the computer had just shown him what had happened to Henry the Navigator, more than sixty years ago.

FIFTEEN

Never

Henry's dreams, that night, were of black skies and black seas, wounded planes and computer screens.

As soon as he woke up, he realised that he must tell Dottie. He had to tell her everything, about all the strange things he'd been hearing and seeing and dreaming. He had to tell her that Simon's great-grandfather, Rusty Dobbs, had been Henry's best friend; that he'd flown with him on twelve missions and had been lucky not to die with him. Most of all, he had to tell her what he knew about Henry the Navigator – that Henry had died bravely.

Dottie needed to know that. There were people alive today, and their children and grandchildren, who didn't know that they owed their lives to Henry, for ditching the Lancaster in the sea. For losing his own life.

'No message. Nothing,' Dottie had said, when she'd told him about Henry.

But Henry the Navigator *had* left a message, Henry was sure. Bits of it were scattered everywhere, waiting to be pieced together and made into sense. And, Henry felt sure, it was for Dottie, not for him; he was just the messenger.

Today was the end of term, he remembered: a special day at school, his last day ever in Year 6. All the same, he wanted to see Dottie first, or at the very least leave a message that he had something important to tell her later. He was ready early, before Dad had picked up his keys and gone out to the car. 'See you later, Dad,' he called, and went along to Pat's.

Something was different. Henry could tell as soon as Pat opened the door. A quietness hung over the house. The postman came up the path behind him, whistling cheerfully, but he too seemed to realise that something was wrong. He handed over a postcard and two letters and went away in silence.

Pat's eyes were rimmed with red and she held a crumpled tissue in one hand. She looked at him vaguely, then said, 'Oh, Henry. We've all had a bit of a shock. I'm afraid poor Dottie passed away in her sleep last night.'

Passed away – that meant – something inside Henry gave a sickening leap. *'No!'* he wanted to shout, but his voice couldn't get past the choking lump in his throat. He stared at Pat to make sure he hadn't mistaken her. She blinked rapidly and made a gulping sound. It was so alarming seeing an adult almost crying that Henry turned away and blundered into the open gate.

'What's up?'

Dad, about to get into his car, stowed his briefcase inside and came over, and Pat had to explain again.

'I'm so sorry,' Dad said, in a quiet, serious voice, putting an arm round Henry's shoulders.

'We've been half expecting it, but all the same—' Pat said. 'Come on in for a minute, won't you?'

They followed her inside without speaking. There was a strange stillness, as if the house knew that something had come to an end. *Passed away,* Henry thought. He knew it was adult-speak for dead, but it sounded different – as if she'd gone on somewhere else, moved on. Henry couldn't imagine Dottie dead. He couldn't take in what it meant.

'What can I do to help?' Dad asked.

'It's all right,' Pat said. 'There's a lot to do, but I can't think about it yet. Stay while I make coffee, if you've got a few minutes.'

Dad nodded. Pat went into the kitchen to fill the kettle; Dad made a quick call on his mobile to say he'd be a bit late for work. Then he said to Henry, 'Poor old Dottie. You'll miss her, won't you?'

Henry couldn't speak. What had happened was so big and so strange that it seemed wrong to chat normally. He wondered if Dottie was lying up there in her bed and he had the idea that if he went up and spoke to her she'd suddenly sit up and have a good idea for a Scrabble word. Then he saw the Scrabble box on a corner table, with its lid on, and Dottie's green knitting rolled up on top of it. It seemed final – the odds and ends of Dottie's life, tidied up. He tried to swallow and couldn't.

Pat came back with mugs of coffee and squash for Henry. 'I called the doctor late last night. I was a bit worried about her, she seemed unconscious rather than asleep, and he arranged for her to be taken straight into hospital. But she passed away without regaining consciousness. John's there now, getting the forms and things.'

'Do you mean,' Henry kept his voice low and respectful, 'do you mean that after I was here yesterday, when it thundered, she was never awake again?'

'I don't think she was. But then—' Pat made an effort to sound more cheerful – 'I don't think she

140

can have known. She just slipped away. It's what she would have wanted – not lingering for months in hospital. She'd have hated that. Grace is out in the garden,' she added. 'Why don't you go outside with your drink? It's a bit gloomy for you in here.'

Henry didn't want to see Grace, but he thought that perhaps Pat wanted him out of the way, so he picked up his glass and went. All he could think was that he'd missed the chance to tell Dottie about Henry's heroic death. She would never know. Never. Never.

Never was too big a word to fit inside his head. Never started now and went on for always.

It was damp and fresh outside after last night's storm, the grass still damp. Grace was kicking a ball about in a half-hearted way, her face tight and scowling. Without even looking at Henry, she said, 'You know about Aunt Dottie?'

'Yes.' He didn't want to talk about it, not to Grace. She'd probably think it was exciting or say horrible things about dead people and funerals. Then she did look at him, and he saw that she had been crying. Really crying: her eyes were red and her nose swollen, and she looked as if she had a streaming cold. Henry thought that perhaps he ought to cry too, but he couldn't. He felt shocked, numb, hollow inside, but not tearful. He was still trying to take in the fact that he'd seen Dottie only the day before yesterday, when she'd talked about coming to the fete, and now she wouldn't be able to go there or anywhere else. Ever.

But she promised, he thought.

There was a gap where Dottie's garden chair should have been. Henry stared at the empty space and saw Grace looking at it too. The whole place felt different without Dottie.

'You know that knitting she was always doing?' Grace said. 'That green thing? It was for me. She was knitting me a jumper. I didn't want it, but now I do. I want her to finish it.' She glared at him. 'I told Mum – I told her—' Her voice wobbled. 'I told her I wouldn't be seen dead in it.' A big tear spilled down her face, then another. She wiped them away, then kicked the football hard into the flower bed, where it snapped a big yellow daisy off its stalk.

'She's great, Aunt Dottie,' she said. 'She doesn't think I'm daft, wanting to be a pilot. She told me, if I want it bad enough, then I'm bound to do it.'

'Yes, I know,' Henry said. 'She told me, too.'

What about me? he was thinking. She'd said that to Grace and was knitting her a jumper, but what had she left for him? Perhaps she only liked me because I reminded her of the other Henry, he thought, and then: how mean, to think that way about someone who's only just died.

Grace picked the football out of the flower bed and wiped bits of damp grass and earth off it. 'I'm going over to see Amber. It's horrible here. Mum says I don't have to go to school. Are you going?'

'Don't know,' Henry said; it had suddenly become a day quite unlike any other.

Grace sniffed and wiped her hand across her nose. 'If you want, in the summer holidays, I'll teach you to ride properly. With a saddle and everything. Not like last time.'

Henry knew it was the closest she would ever get to saying sorry.

'If you like,' he said. 'Thanks.'

It was the closest he could get, too.

SIXTEEN

Promise

Lunch was early on Saturday, because Mum was eager not to miss any of the village fête.

'Are we still going?' Henry asked. 'It doesn't feel right.'

'Henry,' Mum said gently, 'if we could ask Dottie what she wanted you to do, what d'you think she'd say? Would she rather you went to the fête or would she prefer you to hang around indoors feeling miserable?'

Henry thought about it. All yesterday, all today, he'd had a hollow, empty feeling inside, and a sense that something was weighing him down. *This can't be all,* he kept thinking. *This can't be all there is! Someone's here and then gone, leaving nothing.* Into his mind came Dottie's face and her bright eyes looking at him, and her voice saying, 'You go and have a good time! Don't let me stop you, just because I've gone and died.'

He felt more cheerful. 'Go to the fête.'

'Yes, that's what I think. It won't make us forget all about Dottie, but it *will* take our minds off things for a while. And you can't leave a hole in the relay team, can you?'

The fête was behind the village hall, which was decked with coloured flags. Usually empty apart from football goal-posts, the big field was now crammed with a bouncy castle, a large marquee, various stands and stalls, and an agility course for dogs. The running-track had been marked out around the perimeter, roped off. Henry and his parents were among the first to pay their 50ps to go in, but soon the field was crowded with people, some of whom he recognised. There was the postman with his wife, and the lady from the shop, and Elissa with her parents, and Simon with a very bouncy, excitable collie called Pogo. 'He's doing dog agility,' Simon told Henry, 'and I bet he'll win – he's brilliant at it.' Henry's mum, noticing the plant stall, veered off in that direction, while Dad chatted to Simon's Dad, who had just the same fox-red hair as Simon, and Simon demonstrated how Pogo would Sit and Stay on command.

A few minutes later Neil arrived, and the three

boys and Elissa went into a huddle and talked tactics. Henry was to run third, after Neil and Elissa, leaving Simon, the fastest runner, to do the final lap.

'What's the opposition?' Henry asked, since the others were making the race sound very serious indeed.

'The Crickford Cheetahs,' Simon said. 'They're the ones we've got to beat. That's Tim, Grace, Tracy and Dean.'

For a second Henry thought he said Cheaters, only he didn't see how you could cheat in a relay. 'Grace!' he echoed. 'Well, I don't know if she's coming, cos—'

'She's over there.' Simon nodded towards the start. There was Grace, in running shorts and trainers, looking very fit and athletic. Like a winner.

'I didn't know we needed a team name,' Elissa said. 'What's ours?'

Simon grinned. 'I've entered us as the Hurtling Hens.'

'The *what*?' Henry felt himself beginning to go red; he felt betrayed – and by Simon of all people!

'The Hurtling Hens. HENS stands for Henry, Elissa, Neil and Simon. Good, isn't it?' Simon pretended to be a running hen, with chest puffed out and arms held stiffly like wings, legs pumping up and down on the spot. Henry laughed with the others, relieved to be sharing a Hen joke that was nothing to do with him.

'Only don't run like *that.*' Neil poked Simon in the ribs. 'Or we'll come last by miles!'

The sports began with the under-tens and infants – running races, egg-and-spoon, sack races and three-legged races. Henry began to feel nervous as the time drew nearer for his own event. He tightened the laces on his trainers.

'Relay teams,' the loudspeaker said. 'Competitors go to the start, please.'

The number ones lined up, six of them – Neil, Tracy from Grace's team and four boys and a girl Henry didn't know. The others waited by the side of the track, jiggling up and down so that they were ready to run.

'On your marks . . . get set . . . *go!*' shouted the starter, and they were off. Henry felt himself tensed up with eagerness, wanting to run his best, not to let his team down.

Tracy was obviously the weakest runner of the Cheetahs – she was behind almost before they had rounded the first turn – but the other girl pounded strongly ahead, her blonde pony-tail flying out behind. By the first changeover, her team – the Ridgeley Rockets – had a clear lead over Neil in second place, but their next runner wasn't as fast. Elissa, on the second lap for the Hens, had a look of fierce determination that said she was going to catch up or burst a blood vessel in the effort. 'Go, Lissa!' Simon yelled.

Henry took his place, hand outstretched ready for the baton. Elissa pounded towards him, all the time gaining on the boy, her small weight seeming to shake the ground. Henry concentrated hard on the baton – mustn't drop it, mustn't fumble and waste time! – then gripped it surely in his hand and drove himself forward. *'Go* on, Henry!' he heard Dad shout from behind the ropes. The Cheetahs' handover hadn't been so smooth and now Henry found himself running alongside Tim from Grace's team, matching him stride for stride, with the Rockets runner a little behind and the others straggling. It would be Simon and Grace in the final lap; the race would be lost if he didn't keep up.

Henry was straining every muscle, but slowly Tim inched ahead, every stride increasing his lead. Henry felt himself starting to wilt, with nothing more to give. In a second the runner in third place would pass him.

Then a voice yelled out, quite close, 'Get a shift on, Henry! Move yourself! You can do it!'

He could have sworn, just for a baffled second,

that it was Dottie's voice, cracked and old, but rising above the shouts of the other spectators. She was cheering, just for him! There was no time to look round to see where she was, but he felt himself moving up a gear, finding an extra burst of energy as his feet pounded the track. Tim gave him a startled look as he drew level. Held his position. Second place wasn't good enough for the Hens. He wanted to win – win for Dottie.

Simon was waiting, poised, hand stretched out for the baton, Grace next to him almost bursting with impatience. Henry made an extra spurt, found himself overtaking Tim, and even though his lungs felt like bursting, he kept his lead for the final dash. He thrust the baton safely into Simon's hand, watched him sprint off, and stood by the trackside, hands on his knees, panting, but paying close attention to the last lap. 'Well done!' Neil thumped him on the back, and Elissa jumped up and down, saying, 'That was great. We could win this!'

Simon and Grace were running strongly, Simon keeping his lead; the Rockets, not as good as their name, were in third place, and the other three teams hardly in the race at all. Although Grace had longer legs and was taller, Henry could tell from Simon's look of set determination that he wasn't going to let her pass him without a struggle.

'Run, Si!'

'Don't look round! Keep going!'

'Grace! Grace! Come on, Cheetahs!'

'Go for it – you're nearly there!'

It was almost a photo-finish – a few metres more and Grace would have won, but Simon kept up the effort right to the tape, and by sheer willpower managed to keep ahead.

'*Yes! Yes!* We did it! We've won!' Elissa shrieked.

'A very exciting finish there,' came over the loud-speakers, 'with the Hurtling Hens just taking first place from the Crickford Cheetahs, but very well run by both teams.'

For a second Henry caught himself looking round for Dottie, knowing how pleased she'd be, before remembering that of course she wasn't there and couldn't know. A wave of regret washed through him, but there was no time to stop and think, as Grace – Grace! – came over to clap him on the back and say, 'Well done, Strawberry. You did really well.'

It was generous of her, Henry thought, because it was obvious she'd have won if it had been a straight race between her and Simon. 'You too,' he said gruffly.

'Yeah, well. Your team was better.'

Henry wondered what she'd say if he told her

that Dottie had come to cheer him on, just as she'd promised. He scanned the faces of the people standing at the trackside, imagining Dottie's face creasing up with pleasure, grinning in triumph, like when she'd got the eighty-six at Scrabble.

Already competitors were lining up for the sack race. 'Lissa'll win this, you watch,' said Simon, and he was right. By taking quick little steps with her feet pushed to the bottom corners of the sack, Elissa beat all the people who took giant bounds and tired themselves out. Next, there was a slow bicycle race. Henry hadn't tried that, but it looked like fun. Anyone who fell off their bike or had to put a foot on the ground was disqualified. It went on for so long that Simon and Henry got bored and wandered off to the Wellie Whanging, at which Henry's Dad was surprisingly successful.

'Dog Agility is about to begin,' said the commentator (who, Henry had realised, was the man who ran the Post Office). 'Will all dogs wishing to take part please bring their owners to the Dog Agility course.'

Simon went to collect Pogo from his father. It was like TV programmes Henry had seen – the dogs had to weave through poles, leap up to a table and lie down, and go over miniature show jumps. Some of the dogs and owners looked very professional, but others were just having a go, like Simon. He told Henry, 'Pogo's ace at this. Just you watch.'

'Simon Dobbs and Pogo,' called the commentator, and Simon entered the ring with his dog obediently at heel.

'He's very well trained!' said Henry's Mum, who had just joined them, carrying a straw basket full of plants.

'Well, I do my best. The dog's not bad, either,' joked Simon's Dad.

The whistle sounded and Simon set off at a jog, whistling. But the collie was too overwhelmed with excitement even to look at the jumps; he dashed in mad circles, barking, while Simon tried to show him what to do. In the end Simon gave up with Pogo and completed the whole course himself, hurdling jumps, weaving through cones, and even lying on the table while the collie looked on in puzzlement. Everyone applauded wildly as Simon left the ring, very red in the face, with Pogo bounding beside him looking as pleased as if he'd done everything perfectly.

'You want to enter that lad for Crufts,' one of the dog-handlers said to Simon's Dad.

Henry's Dad slipped him a two-pound coin. 'Go and buy ice-creams for yourself and Simon. He looks as if he could do with one.'

'I'll take Pogo,' offered Simon's Dad. 'Course, it'd have been different with me in charge. Knows his master's voice, that dog.'

'Stage-fright,' Simon told him, 'that's all it was. Dad, is it OK if Henry comes round tomorrow?'

'Course,' said Simon's Dad. 'Tomorrow afternoon? Gran and Grandad'll be there as well.'

As he and Simon crossed the field to the ice-cream van, Henry thought of all the things he had to look forward to. It was the summer holidays now, and he was going to Simon's, and Grace was going to teach him to ride properly. In two weeks' time he was going to Scotland with Mum and Dad, and when they got back Nabil was coming to stay. At the end of it would be school, but he needn't worry about that yet, and anyway he had friends who would be just as new as he was. He'd run well in the race and – he couldn't be certain, but he felt fairly sure – he'd grown a little bit taller, just a tiny bit, since they'd come to live in the village. When they got home, he'd ask Mum to make a new pencil mark on his bedroom doorframe, so that he could keep a check.

He looked across the field to the line of roofs and chimneys that was Church Cottages and home, and felt for the first time that he belonged here.

SEVENTEEN

Rusty's Luck

Simon's house was in Upper Crickford, a few miles away, and was one of a pair of farm cottages, with flinty walls. Everyone was in the garden – garden-living had become normal, this long, hot summer. Henry wondered what it would feel like to go back to rooms and sofas and fires.

In all the excitement of the fête, he'd forgotten that Simon's great-grandad was Rusty Dobbs, but remembered in the instant of meeting.

Rusty Dobbs had grey hair, but otherwise looked like a much older version of Simon. He didn't look nearly as old as Dottie. Henry realised that it must have been Dottie's illness that made her so old and frail, but Rusty Dobbs could hardly have looked healthier. He played boisterous games with Pogo, told lots of jokes and laughed loudly at them. His wife, Simon's geat-grandmother, had just come from the swimming-pool, and her hair was still wet.

When, for a moment, Rusty and Simon and Simon's dad all stood together admiring the runner-beans, Henry had the odd feeling of looking at a family of Russian dolls, all with the same smile. Just for a second, he thought of another family – Henry the Navigator, grey like Rusty, and Dottie, and someone around Dad's age, and a boy of about ten, and a little girl in a pushchair. The family that never was, he thought. The family-to-be, that crashed into the sea with Henry.

Rusty Dobbs was amazed when Henry told him who Dottie was. He stared and stared, then shook his head like a dog shaking water out of its ears after a swim.

'Yes, I remember Dottie all right,' he told Henry, suddenly sounding much younger. 'Lovely girl, she was – those blue, blue eyes, I remember, and that laugh! I always claimed it was me saw her first—'

'You watch what you say!' said Simon's gran.

'That was before I'd met Mary, of course.' Rusty gave one of his grins and took her hand. 'But Dottie only had eyes for Henry. And you mean she's been over in Crickford St. Thomas the last few weeks and I could have gone over and had a good old natter? And now it's too late?'

'She'd have loved that,' Henry said sadly. 'Talking about Henry.'

'Sad. Sad.' Rusty was silent for a few moments; then he said: 'Still, I'll go and pay my last respects. Buy her a big bunch of flowers. You must get Simon to bring you round to our house some time,' he added. 'We're in Stowmarket. I've got loads of photos I can show you. There's quite a few of Henry.' Then he gave Henry a sideways look. 'You know what? You remind me of him.'

'Dottie said that,' Henry told him.

'Yes, I can see why. Same dark hair, same eyes, same look. No wonder you brought all the old memories back, for Dottie. I'll always remember him – a good mate, he was. Tell you what,' said Rusty. He reached into the back pocket of his trousers and pulled out his wallet. 'I'm going to give you something. Something of his, to keep.'

Henry could feel his heart beating. In the second before he saw it – something Rusty Dobbs kept in his wallet, in a screw of paper – he knew what it would be.

Henry's sixpence. The sixpenny-bit Henry had given Rusty the very first time they'd seen Dottie.

'You can't give me that!' Henry burst out. 'It's yours. For luck—'

Rusty gave him a curious stare. 'Well, how d'you

know that? You're right, though. Henry gave it me and told me to keep it for good luck. And I always have. Now I reckon it's your turn.' He put the coin in the palm of Henry's hand.

'What's that?' Simon came over to look.

It still looked shiny and new. It showed the head of King George and the date, 1943. It had been in Henry the Navigator's pocket and could easily have been spent at the canteen. But it had become Rusty's Luck.

'Wait!' Henry protested. 'What if *your* luck runs out, if you give it to me?'

'Well, you know?' Rusty gave a contented chuckle, and looked around the garden, then up at the sky, then at Simon. 'I reckon I've had all the luck I could ever want, in my life. Now it's your turn. You keep it, lad.' He took the coin back, rewrapped it in its twist of paper, and handed it to Henry. Henry put it carefully in his shorts pocket.

'Thank you,' he said. 'Thanks a million.'

It didn't seem enough.

What if Henry had kept it for himself, he wondered? Would things have been different? Surely not. It was only a coin. But he was going to keep it carefully, keep it always. He would find it a special place.

'Tea's ready!' shouted Simon's Dad from the

patio. There was a garden table laid with big plate-fuls of sandwiches and scones and doughnuts. Sud-denly, Henry was ravenous.

'Jam doughnuts! My favourite,' said Rusty Dobbs.

When he got home, the first thing Henry saw was Dottie's Scrabble box on the table.

'Pat brought it round,' Mum explained. 'She thought you might like to have something of Dottie's, to keep.'

EIGHTEEN

At the Firefly Gate

Henry was too excited to sleep.

He kept reliving the events of the past two days – Rusty Dobbs, the race, Dottie's voice coming to him from nowhere, the surge of energy that pushed him towards the winning tape. He wouldn't have believed it if the red certificate – First Place, Relay – hadn't been propped against the bookshelf, with his name on it along with Simon's, Ellie's and Neil's. They'd been given one each.

It wasn't fully dark. The bedroom curtains stirred in a faint breeze, and through them he could see the almost-lightness of a summer night that would soon turn to early dawn. Henry thought of the strange night when he'd lain in bed and listened to the Lancaster bombers flying overhead, out to-wards the sea. And not just heard them, but seen them; or if not, it had been an extraordinarily vivid dream.

He didn't think he'd carry on seeing and hearing things any more.

Dottie's funeral was to be held on Thursday, in the village church. 'Not a very nice start to the summer holidays for you,' Mum had said. 'You don't have to come if you don't want to.'

Henry didn't know whether he wanted to go or not. He didn't like the idea of a funeral. There would be lots of people and flowers and there was a proper way of doing it, all solemn and dignified, but it wouldn't have much to do with Dottie.

'Oh, I can't be doing with all that fuss,' he imagined her saying.

But Rusty Dobbs was going. Henry was pleased about that. It seemed right; a proper ending to something that had taken all these years to reach an end. In a way, Rusty would be saying a final goodbye to Henry. Rusty had had all the luck and Henry the Navigator hadn't. Now it was Henry's turn to keep Rusty's lucky sixpence. Mum had found some special silver-polish; now, as bright and shiny as in his dream, the sixpence was on his bedside table, next to his lamp, where he could keep looking at it.

Henry thought about Rusty's bout of flu. If only

Henry had caught it too! Then his story and Dottie's could have had a different ending.

And if Rusty Dobbs hadn't caught the flu, Henry wouldn't have Simon for a friend.

He hadn't told Simon, yet, about all the things he knew; maybe he never would. Perhaps it was meant to be his secret; his and Dottie's. And Henry's.

He threw back his duvet and slid out of bed, feeling the warm smoothness of floorboards with his feet. Dottie's Scrabble set was on top of his chest of drawers. He hadn't yet opened it, but now he lifted the lid, took out the board and put out one letter-rack. Would the letters still say anything that made sense, now that Dottie had gone?

Closing his eyes, he picked seven tiles, as if getting ready to play a game all by himself.

U B K E L Y C

He hardly needed to start moving them around before he saw what they spelled out.

BE LUCKY.

Thank you, he said silently.

He went to the window and opened it wide. Night-time smells wafted in – mown grass and roses and the honey-sweet smell of the lime trees in front of the Old Rectory. Somewhere, over the fields, a bird screeched.

He couldn't see them at first; then they started to appear, one by one, like someone lighting tiny candles. The fireflies, dancing round the gate as if showing the way.

Someone was walking towards the gate, beneath the trees. Henry stared, his eyes making out shapes through the twisted branches. Hunched shoulders, hands deep in pockets. Feet walking as far as the gate, then stopping. A face in profile, looking to-wards the Old Rectory.

Henry's haunt! Henry was waiting for Dottie at the firefly gate, still waiting, keeping the promise he had kept for years. But he couldn't know that Dottie wasn't here any more.

Am I dreaming or am I awake? Henry wondered how he could tell. On an impulse, he leaned farther out of the window. 'Henry!' he shouted.

For an instant the young man's face turned in his direction. Then another voice called out, 'Henry!' from the village end of the orchard, and both Henrys turned to look.

Dottie was running along the path, her long hair streaming.

Henry knew it was Dottie. It was the girl he had seen at the canteen van; the girl of the orchard; the girl with the amazing blue eyes, though he couldn't see them now. She wore the sky-blue dress with the white collar, and her feet were in white plimsolls. She ran as lightly as a moth skimming the grass, the skirt of her dress floating out like papery wings.

Henry the Navigator held out his arms to her, and for a moment the two figures were locked together in the middle of the firefly dance.

Then they moved away, arm-in-arm, talking, beneath the trees.

Dottie laughed, a mischievous giggle that rippled into Henry's ears, as her blue dress faded like smoke beneath the apple trees.

'Goodbye, Dottie,' he whispered.

But she had gone.